I0396965

MANAGING

MANAGEMENT

~

Nick S Dyer was at sea for the first seven years of his working life; he trained as a steam engineer on a salvage tug.

After becoming a land lover, he worked as a nightclub bouncer, a prison officer and made several short films for the BBC. Nick has lectured on a variety of subjects at Worcester Cathedral, Oxford University and at Buckingham Palace in the presence of Her Royal Highness the Princess Royal. He is now retired and living in Worcestershire.

Nick's ambitions are to write because people actually enjoy reading his work and live for so many years he becomes a wrinkled, wizened, grumpy old reprobate. Some would say he is well on the way to achieving the latter of these desires.

~

By the same author

TOBY DICKINSON'S NEW DIMENSIONS
The first book of the Daurth chronicles

TOBY DICKINSON'S STRANDS OF TIME
The second book of the Daurth chronicles

TOBY DICKINSON'S TRANSPAR INHERITANCE
The third book of the Daurth chronicles

TOBY DICKINSON'S DARKLIN CONSEQUENCE
The fourth book of the Daurth chronicles

TOBY DICKINSON'S MULTIVERSE OF TIME
The fifth book of the Daurth chronicles

POETRY, MY VERSION
(Out of print)

POETRY MY SECOND VERSION
(Moods for another time)

Non-fiction

FIRST RESORTS FROM A LAST RESORT
A proposition of mandatory systems in the workplace

PHILOSOPHY FOR THE BEAST
A view of what the world needs to be

AN AMERICAN JOURNAL
Ten thousand miles by car and train across the USA

MANAGING

MANAGEMENT

NICK S DYER

First Published by WFA Publishing July 1998
Published in hardback by LULU PUBLISHING November 2009
This edition published by LULU PUBLISHING December 2013

Order this book online at www.nicksdyer.com , from all major online
book retailers and www.lulu.com

ISBN: 978-1-291-64797-6

Dedications & Thanks

For every manager who ever thought that they needed a friend, perhaps this book might be one.

My thanks must go to all the bad managers; they probably made me look better than I may have been.

~

CONTENTS

~

<u>Introduction</u>

The problem with many publications and tutorials about management is they lack pragmatism, that sadder but wiser feeling. A cynical realism and the coping humour experienced managers need in order to retain their sanity is invariably missing.

The following pages will realistically equip junior managers by giving them an overview only experience can bring. These folios will also assist senior managers to keep their sense of proportion and revitalise their modus operandi.

The job of a manager was never more complex. The burden placed upon people in charge today has never been so demanding. There is the continual desire to obtain more for less at greater speed whilst still raising standards.

Political correctness accompanied by more employment legislation than ever waits to destroy the careers of the unprepared and ill-equipped. Pragmatic understanding of management and simplistic ways of coping are more necessary now than ever; you will find them within these chapters.

I realised a long time ago that psychology is not the exclusive realm of the academic or intellectual; it is the study of human beings and seeks to give explanations for our behaviour. No manager will ever administer people successfully without some accurate understanding of human behaviour and basic psychological theorem.

Psychologists should never be confused with the medical profession of psychiatrists. A psychiatrist is a medical practitioner that some managers may end up seeing, perhaps because they failed to read a copy of this book!

1

What is a manager?

Over the years, many experts have defined the facets that make a manager. They still cannot agree exactly what all those facets are. Conceivably, successful managers must be everything experts say and more. Perhaps no one should argue about a defining list, but merely contribute to it ad-infinitum…

- Management has parental aspects

- A manager must be firm

- A manager must be flexible

- Management is about organisation

- Managers are team builders

- Good managers must be leaders

- Management is a lonely place

- Managers must be lateral thinkers

- Management requires self-realisation

- A good manager finds staff that cover his or her weaknesses

- A manager needs to be both pro-active and reactive

- Managers should not be control freaks

- Management should be supportive

- Managers should delegate not abdicate

- Managers must be able to…

The list is perhaps, endless. For every bullet point above, I expect most managers could add another; I probably would not disagree with any of them. However, far more important than statements describing what a manager should be, is identifying and understanding an overall philosophy of managing.

- Objectives, an energetic belief, coupled with a systematic common sense approach, are the beginnings of managerial achievement

The Philosophy Of Managing

The difference between common sense and wisdom is not easily defined – the two attributes tend to overlap in many ways.

Wisdom usually stands for an accumulation of knowledge and then its skilful application; it is often associated with the older person, whereas common sense can be exhibited at any age. Clearly though, the wise have common sense and the use of common sense proclaims at least a measure of wisdom.

No matter what their age, managers require a quantity of both attributes if they are to be successful.

- The most important qualification that any manager can have is common-sense

- An ounce of common-sense is worth a pound of academic qualification

Any company or organisation must have a clear statement of what they want to achieve, for example…

Ford wants to produce a thousand motorcars a week. The cars must be made to a stated level of quality. H.M. Prison Service wants to keep everyone committed to prison by the courts in safe and secure custody. They require convicted prisoners to address their offending behaviour.

It does not matter what aims or objectives an organisation may have, how simple or complex, as long as the management of that company have clearly identified what those objectives are. The next step is to decide how aims will be achieved – this seems to be where mistakes begin.

Often managers do not agree about the way to the metaphoric 'promised land' of fulfilled targets. If clear mandatory systems of operation do not exist within an organisation, then progress depends almost entirely on the entrepreneurial whim of an individual manager. If the said manager is brilliant, then the company succeeds and enjoys huge profits/achievements. However, what happens if that manager leaves?

Many managers progress through a company's promotion structure by being able to say, *'See the way that works? I created that!'* Fine! All organisations need change and innovation, but they do not need change for changes sake. Neither should companies be run according to personal likes, dislikes, or perhaps worst of all, the vain insecurities of narcissistic managers who long to create something in their own image.

- Lasting success only comes from sound system and structure

Entrepreneurs are very necessary people. The economic structure of the world would probably collapse without them. Nevertheless, eventually any good entrepreneur will take his innovation, turn it into a system of best practice and dedicate it to a business; if not, someone else will; if that does not happen, failure will follow.

Managers are not entrepreneurs. Entrepreneurs might be managers, but unless they are managing their own 'one-man-band', their management skills are usually abysmal. Consider the following organization…

McDonalds

This company has achieved worldwide success by dedicating a realistic system of best practice all over the world since 1940.

A McDonald's restaurant is recognisable no matter in which country it might be located. Managers gain reward within the organisation not by tearing down and rebuilding in their own image, but by preserving and nurturing a winning system.

Innovation and ideas continue to flow in abundance, but they are developed in a structured way. Improvements are introduced on a worldwide scale, usually on the same day; that is system and structure operating at its best.

HM Prison Service

This organisation suffers considerably from conflicting philosophies. On the one hand, the Prison Service probably has more rules – which suggest system and structure – than most any other three organisations put together. On the other hand, the Service is blighted by a desire to let managers manage in their own individualistic, entrepreneurial, way.

Constantly senior management twist or even ignore rules and literally, do their own thing.

The Prison Service struggles to introduce something new into all jails in the same year, let alone the same day. Aims and objectives constantly lack systematic application, are often unrealistic, and consequently very often disregarded.

Managers habitually tear down the work of their predecessors only to rebuild the same thing a few years later when somebody convinces somebody else it is their new idea.

- A manager must systemise all plans designed to achieve aims and objectives

- Systems must be realistic structures that everyone understands and supports

- Once a system is in place, there must be no individual alterations allowed

- Changes to a system must be organisationally sanctioned, properly planned and realistically resourced

Think about your personal life, your habits at home, your customs and practice, what you do every morning. You probably get up, use the bathroom, get dressed, have breakfast and go to work. If you wrote that routine down, it would obviously be simplistic, but nonetheless, a recognisable system.

Try varying what you do every morning. Do not use the bathroom, just start eating breakfast. Better still, don't bother getting dressed, go to work, as you are; ridiculous? Of course it would be. Then why are so many organisations conducting business in a similar manner?

Nobody can live their lives without some degree of systematic custom and practice. And nobody can manage a business without clear systems of practice, but those systems must be recorded and mandatory or they become vulnerable to the vagaries of unwritten custom and the whim of individual likes and dislikes.

- Managers need systems of working for all their staff

- Systems must be recorded, visible and accessible

- Systems must only be altered on a company-wide basis

- Entrepreneurial innovation must be structured

A manager must possess energetic belief – a conviction in what he or she is doing, together with the vigour to carry it through. They must also possess self-belief as well. If they are not convinced of their own attributes, how will they inspire confidence in others?

Managers are often told they should be dynamic. Perhaps energetic is a better term, especially when linked with the beliefs and philosophy of management.

The word dynamic has a propensity towards the individualistic, whereas energetic expresses more positive plural connotations. Enthusing people with your positive belief in a system creates an energy that becomes infectious. Achieving requires energy and it is a manager's job to provide that force.

Self-belief is an absolute necessity. Nobody can ever be a successful manager if they do not have confidence in themselves. Self-belief provides a manager with the confidence to operate positively, even under adversity.

A manager must always provide the foundation of confidence from which his/her staff can function.

- Self-belief is not always being right and never accepting that someone else can have a better idea

- Self-belief is being confident enough to admit you can be wrong

- Self-belief is being secure in self and others

- Self-belief is appearing calm in the face of adversity

- Self-belief is a willingness to always face issues and solve problems

The philosophy of managing is more important than any of the things a manager is or is not supposed to be. The philosophy declares attributes a manager will need and how those attributes should be employed. However, despite the extensive list at the start and the all-encompassing philosophy, perhaps the question posed at the beginning of this chapter still lacks a specific answer.

What is a manager? The answer is amazingly simple and sums up the philosophy in one short sentence. No matter what his or her level of seniority in an organisation, **a manager is a facilitator**, nothing more, nothing less.

Anything, or anyone, being managed is being managed for a purpose, to either produce or achieve something. In order to produce or achieve, workers are needed.

A manager **facilitates** production and achievement by **facilitating** the workers' abilities to complete the required tasks.

If managers ever lose sight of what their job really is, they cease to be effective.

2

Communications

Many managers seriously underestimate the value of good communications. Some pay communications expensive lip service and produce internal papers or magazines. There maybe company memos that go to every department and often get dumped, emails that are disregarded, or an intranet staff use selectively.

Most managers do not communicate properly with the most valuable asset they possess – their staff.

- Always remember, the first rule of communication is listening

- If you do not listen, you do not communicate, just dictate

Internal papers or magazines can be useful, but merely as a secondary way of informing. All too often, such company media is seen as nothing more than boring facts and figures, no matter how well presented, or even worse as a propaganda sheet from a remote management: they lack dynamism, editorial realism and only the most motivated, or sycophantic, read them completely.

E-mails or other IT systems are little better and should never be depended upon – except as a vehicle for an office joker. Memos frequently attain the importance they deserve only after rumour has provided a damaging exaggeration of content.

Some organisations have written staff suggestion schemes. Such systems can be successful and produce good ideas, but they have a serious down side.

If any idea submitted fails to receive a reply, the staff member concerned often feels ignored and unappreciated. Written suggestion schemes frequently become the conduit for anonymous abuse, senior management invariably under value the system once that happens.

- The written word should only be a way of reinforcing verbal communications

- Communication within an organisation should always begin verbally

Verbal communication is one of the most important tools of a good manager. It provides the opportunity to discover what the workforce thinks, not only by listening to them, but by observing their non-verbal communications.

Non-verbal communication is one of the best ways to form an opinion about what a person honestly feels because much of it is done unconsciously.

In a formal situation, answers may well be guarded; an employee's stance is often stilted and unnatural. Informally, a perceptive manager may deduce a more accurate picture. Not from what the employee states, but from the way they say it.

- When a manager speaks to a member of staff formally it should be in the manager's environment

A manager's office ought to be personalised. It then becomes their territory, their individualistic sanctum. Psychologically, whoever enters your environment is at a disadvantage. When trying to cultivate a relaxed situation, communicate with staff in a neutral area or their workplace.

Your office takes them from their comfort zone; the familiar workplace provides an employee with an unconscious sense of security.

- Only communicate formally when the situation dictates there is no alternative

- Informal communication will always yield more information

When communicating with staff, a manager must always be honest. Even good liars are found out eventually.

One deceitful word can cost a manager his credibility, perhaps forever. If you do not know something, say so, or if a matter cannot be discussed, then tell staff exactly that. Although those answers are far from satisfactory, they are better than pretence and will probably gain you more respect.

- Are your staff saying what they believe you want to hear but thinking something else?

- How does their demeanour appear?

- What is their eye contact like?

There are many good books describing the psychological aspects and skills of verbal and non-verbal communication that I would urge any manager to read however, I do not intend to reproduce them here. Many are specialised and have limited fields of suitability.

This chapter will help equip any manager to a competent level, no matter what his or her area of endeavour.

- Day-to-day informal communication between management and staff is essential

- If day-to-day communications do not exist within an organisation, then unions and the verbose will usually fill the communication gap, habitually in a negative way

- Communication is a two-way thing, both parties learn something. What you learn depends on how well you plan your communications

- Communication always facilitates learning; be sure that your staff learn exactly what you mean

When managers communicate with employees, they should always have objectives in mind. They should have a clear idea about what they want to find out and what they want to convey.

Even if the objective is a simple one – perhaps to ensure a member of staff is well – nevertheless, it should be thought out consciously with overall targets in mind.

By keeping the simple rule of having pre-determined objectives in mind, you professionalise thinking and communication skills.

Strive continually to obtain useful knowledge and to impart correct information. Amongst other things, having pre-ordained objectives when communicating allows focus when speaking.

Feedback

Managers expect staff to listen to them, but listening is not enough. Managers should require feedback.

Feedback allows a manager to discover how staff think – how they reach a conclusion – it goes further than an ordinary reply. Feedback means you require focused information about what you say.

- Probably the most important aspect of feedback is to ensure staff understand what you mean

There is often a difference between a literal connotation and an actual meaning. Clearly, *'put the kettle on'* does not usually mean wear a small metal object with a handle and spout on part of one's anatomy.

The phrase obviously implies, *'make a hot drink,'* or perhaps more accurately, expresses a need for some boiling water.

Will a similar, less well-known, idiom of vague meaning cause confusion when a manager gives an instruction to a member of staff? Not if the manager requires feedback.

- If line managers find they do not have time to talk with subordinates every day, then they are not doing their job correctly

- Managers are frequently the centre of attention when among the workforce and must always be aware of what they communicate

- The sub-conscious non-verbal communication syndrome works both ways; constantly be aware of what you say non-verbally

- What managers think they say and what their staff think they say are often two entirely different things

- Requiring feedback ensures everyone understands the correct meaning of what is communicated

- Assumption is the mother and father of most blunders

Personalising Space

Personalise your space; it becomes your foundation of confidence and power when the going gets tough.

The psychological advantage that a personalised office attains can be manipulated to assist certain tasks that a manager is obliged to perform.

How the furniture is placed has an effect and communicates subliminally. Your desk and chair facing the door gives an impression of alertness and confidence in dealing with any problem coming your way. Facing a wall, corner, or having your back to the door implies a desire to hide away and a reluctance to face things.

A carpet or rug suggests a degree of warmth; tiles or vinyl floor covering suggest coldness. Family pictures illustrate warmth and caring. Awards and certificates depict professionalism, position and ability.

For maximum formality, a manager should be seated behind his or her desk. The manager's chair should be slightly higher than the one designated for an employee.

The desk provides a barrier of formality. The lower chair invariably develops a degree of unconscious inferiority within the member of staff. Such a setup is ideal when engaged in disciplinary procedures, but beware, in some situations it could be seen as distant and intimidating, or even provoking and confrontational.

Where possible, interviewing should be conducted in a relaxed manner. Instead of having a chair behind the desk, a manager should bring it to the side eliminating any suggestion of a barrier.

All the seats in the office ought to be of the same height. The manager retains the psychological advantage of his own surroundings, but in a more tranquil situation.

Geographical openness engenders warmth and some accessibility rather than defensiveness or inapproachability.

Interviewing

- All interviews should be planned

- Interviews should be time bound

Any activity benefits from a quantity of forward planning and interviewing is no exception. It is important that, from the beginning, the difference between interviewing and other forms of communication is established.

No matter how supportive and positive, or draconian and negative, all interviews are a formal procedure: they should be recorded and take place in an area set aside for such formality.

Interviews must be devoid of interruption and given a befitting level of importance that is apparent to everyone concerned.

A manager is obliged to control communication during an interview. Probably the best controlling device is open and closed questioning.

- A closed question requires nothing more than a simple yes or no answer. *'Is your name Joe Blogs?'* or *'Do you like the weather today?'*

- An open question requires more information and cannot be answered by a yes or no. *'What is your name?'* or *'What weather do you like?'*

By using open questions, an interviewer can encourage a reluctant talker. Closed questions can be used to inhibit verbosity.

Probably a diplomatic and useful way of shutting up the longwinded is a 'feeding back' interruption consisting of a confirming closed question. *'So actually, your full name is Josie Archibald Blogs isn't it?'* or *'You couldn't care less about the weather could you?'*

The same open technique encourages focused communication from the reticent.

Interviews consist of three parts:

- The introduction

- Information conveying and gathering

- Termination

Introductions vary depending on the type of interview being conducted. However, some procedures apply on any occasion. Everyone present should be introduced and their particular roles explained.

The person being interviewed should be told what the interview is for, even if they already know. Such procedure allows for clear records, complete understanding and the setting of parameters.

Information conveying and gathering, or the second part of the interview, is the element requiring the most planning and dialogue skills. It is very easy to be side-tracked from the goals of an interview, especially if the person speaking is an attractive talker and engages your interest.

A manager must remain focused and be prepared to steer the conversation back on track if required. Remember though, no one can plan for every eventuality. Perhaps something being discussed is more relevant than at first considered so flexibility is required; it is a matter of balance and judgement.

Termination is more than ending the interview because time has run out or you have the answers required. Termination is about ensuring the interviewee leaves the room in the most positive frame of mind possible. Poorly ended interviews can damage a manager's credibility and leave an employee with unproductive frustrations.

Consider the following questions...

- Did the interviewee understand everything said?

- Did the interviewee have a fair chance to say everything he or she wanted?

- Did you understand the interviewee correctly?

- If the time allowed was not enough, was a date set for another interview?

- Did you get all the information you wanted?

- Did you communicate all the information you planned to convey?

- Was a record made of the interview for future reference?

If you answer yes to all the above questions, then no matter what the outcome, the best possible interview will have taken place.

If you answer no anywhere, it is reasonable to assume some kind of failure has occurred or a future problem has been created.

Non-verbal communication during interviews:

- A manager must always be conscious of his or her non-verbal communications during any dialogue.

- Our non-verbal communications are constantly saying something

- Interviews are more acute areas for subconscious perceptions

Interviewing someone for a job with your head stuck constantly in their career history might make you an expert on their past but it will not tell you much about the present. Such a lack of eye contact will however convey a very negative opinion to the prospective employee.

If a manager appears nervous or overawed by any situation during interviews, their demeanour will be conveyed to the interviewee.

The employee's disposition will almost certainly emulate the managers; probably multiplied by a factor of ten!

- During interviews always appear confident

- Convey a pleasant demeanour

- Engage eye contact whenever you speak

- Reward the interviewee's disclosure by visibly paying attention and acknowledging

Listening is not a passive activity. A good listener promotes disclosure from an interviewee by actively communicating non-verbally.

Eye contact, nods, smiles or sympathetic expressions in the right place all reward disclosure.

- Human beings require reward for disclosure

- Consider how you feel when you talk to someone and they are apparently, not paying attention

Remember that if your career blossoms, you will inevitably attend promotion boards or interviews. Some preparation before such occasions is an absolute must.

Obviously, you will need to study the, possibly unique, subject matter from which questions may emerge. However, preparation should include rehearsing some subtle rules that are consistent for any interviewee.

- First appearances do matter tremendously

No matter what your normal dress code, when you attend an interview, especially for advancement, make an observable effort. Nothing creates a better impression than someone who is clean and smart.

When invited to sit down make sure your posterior goes all the way to the back of the chair; such an action achieves two things…

- By placing your bottom at the back of a chair, you will automatically sit in an upright position

- You achieve an open stance. It is not a natural or easy act to cross arms or legs when seated right back in a chair and either action is undesirable

Crossed legs can denote nerves, insecurities or defensiveness. On certain occasions, leg crossing can even be construed as provocative.

Arms crossed or placed in a hugging position around the torso announce defensiveness and a lack of confidence that will probably never inspire a promotion board to place their trust in you.

- How you look often affects the way you feel

- If you look smart and alert you usually are

Most promotion boards consist of more than one person, the popular number in many organisations is three.

Boards sometimes sit behind a long table and the individual in the middle usually acts as a chairperson.

On other occasions, interviews loosely described as, 'the country house chat', are utilised. Apparently laced with informality, everyone concerned usually sits in comfortable soft furnishings in no discernable order.

Plush surroundings away from the workplace can easily cloud issues and professionalism within the interviewee.

* Whatever the format used by interviewers, the interviewee's demeanour should always remain the same

Eye contact and how you use it is most important. If there are three people on a board, it is best to engage eye contact with whomever speaks to you. However, when you answer the person speaking, be sure to attempt eye contact with the other two as well.

By non-verbally communicating with all three people, you make them feel included. The person who asked a question knows you are taking notice when you deliver your verbal answer. By ensuring eye contact with everyone as you speak, they will feel your answer was for all of them.

- Eye contact can speak as loudly as any word and mean twice as much

The philosophical and psychological preciousness of human beings when communicating should never be forgotten. Whatever we say can have a completely different effect depending on how we say it and whom we say it to.

One can amuse, offend, inform, bore and anger different people by delivering the same sentence. Consider this example...

'Starkville Wanderers won the cup!'

- One person found it amusing; he did not believe it could happen in a million years

- The second was offended; she supported the other team and assumes you are making fun and 'winding her up'

- The third person did not know and was therefore informed

- The fourth felt bored, he already knew and hates football

- Another lost twenty pounds betting on the other team he feels angry when reminded

Communicating is one of the most important things a manager does; how they do it can make or break them. Probably the best advice on the subject, are the words of the late Professor Abraham O'Dare...

'Be sure your brain is working before your mouth is; think about what the body parts that can't speak might be saying!'

3

Management and Leadership

The Duke of Wellington once remarked when remonstrating with a less than dynamic officer.

'Go back to your quarter-mastering where you manage most prettily; that just requires books. Leadership requires swords and bold thinking!'

In two short sentences, the Iron Duke gave a good indication of the differences between management and leadership; undoubtedly opposite ends of a wide spectrum.

In order for managers to be successful, they must possess aspects of both attributes. The required percentages of each quality depend upon what is being supervised.

Possibly the Armed Forces, Police, Fire, Prison and Ambulance Services require more leadership from their managers than Tesco Supermarkets or The County Library Service.

- Management is a skill, leadership a quality

- Managers are taught, leaders are born

Psychologists, professors and tacticians have written many books describing the differences between managers and leaders. To have both traits in a person is exceptional.

Winston Churchill was a great leader, but considered a poor manager, as was the Duke of Wellington. On the other hand, there are extremely competent managers who have the leadership skills of a dead cod.

Rather than attempting to name the different components of management and leadership, it might be better if just the main distinction between the two is examined...

- Leadership is management under adversity

Whenever a manager is faced with adverse circumstances that involve other people needing direction, leadership is required. An extreme example is when directly commanding armed forces on active service.

However, if most managerial posts were examined, few would be found completely free from adversity.

Eventually, the crunch comes in any field of endeavour. Decisions need to be made quickly and people need telling decisively what they should do. At some time, all managers need to be a leader.

Habitually, leadership is something many managers fail to exhibit. Some lack the ability, but many are discouraged from showing such intrinsic worth in the first place.

Discouragement comes from above in many organisations; although frequently, it comes from within.

- Managers can be innocuous; leaders are not

- Managers maybe indecisive, a leader can never afford to be

- Many managers are sycophants, leaders rarely are

- Metaphorically, management is from an ivory tower, leadership a bloody field

- Good managers are astute, good leaders courageous

- Leaders make senior managers nervous

- Leadership carries more risk than management

- Nobody likes adversity

- Everyone is an expert when the adversity ceases

- Professor retrospect is the brightest of us all

- Some senior managers resent juniors who think for themselves

- The buck stops with more leaders than managers

Leadership is a risky business. Depending on the level of adversity faced and how fast decisions are required determines the level of risk. Sooner or later, if someone makes enough choices, one of those decisions will be wrong.

Leadership is far more stressful than management and often more thankless. Sometimes, the wisest thing a manager can do is nothing at all. However, not many leaders subscribe to such a policy; inaction is no friend to them.

- Leaders are more liked and respected than managers

- There are more remembered leaders than managers

- Management is almost entirely proactive

- Leadership is often completely reactive

Not just the extremes of adversity require leadership. Taking staff forward into any new field of endeavour and providing detailed planning and guidance, with all the responsibility that entails, requires some aspects of leadership.

- Visible management, willingness to accept responsibility and be accountable, is leadership by any other name

There are no model personality characteristics that persist in leaders. In fact, the opposite appears true.

Throughout history, leaders are noted for being completely different to each other. What they appear to have in common is the charisma to inspire and get the best out of people.

- The qualities exhibited by successful leaders regularly reoccur

All leaders…

- Have clear beliefs and standards

- Stand up for their beliefs

- Are very genuine

- Strive never to deceive

- Are unswerving with both word and deed

- Challenge what they feel is wrong

- Attempt to improve everything

- Are persuasive

- Encourage people to do better

- Know how to build teams

- Know how to inspire ownership

- Know how to delegate

- Know how to listen

- Know their success relies considerably on the work of others

- Give recognition and celebrate success

- Know how to say thank you

Historians repeatedly say that managers are appointed but leaders emerge. Such a theory perhaps reflects how men and women placed in charge tend to use their power and either motivate or compel people to do their jobs.

- Some lead by charismatic personality; they have inspirational characteristics which attract others

- Some manage by high position of power; the overall authority to hire, sack, reward and punish

Without doubt, the best managers are people who can combine the use of both personality and position to influence their subordinates.

Professor O'Dare observes…

'The best leaders are tempered with courage, the caution of good managerial legerdemain and the wisdom to demonstrate both abilities on precisely the right occasions.'

~

4

Change

Ask how many certainties there are in life and most people will say two – birth and death. That answer is incorrect, there are very definitely three. Birth, death, and in between? Change! An undoubtable certainty.

- Change is the third certainty in life

Unlike birth and death, change is always with us and impacts on everything we do. Yet if asked, most people do not know how many types of change there are, how those types of change work, or how to successfully understand and manipulate those categories of change.

Change is something managers must often implement. However, can you apply change with maximum efficiency and success if you do not fully understand how it works? The answer is both obvious and negative.

Remember, managers should never empower their staff to complete a task if they have not first equipped them to do the job. But are you, as a manager, equipped to manage change properly?

- Do you know how many types of change there are?

- Do you know how those different kinds of change work?

- Do you understand what can go wrong with change and why?

If your answer is no to any of the above questions, then you need to study this subject carefully.

You never know, it could get you promoted, save your company money and cut down the stress of managing change in both your professional and personal life forever.

Accepting change as a cast iron certainty allows us to realise the tremendous ongoing impact it has on our lives. Not understanding the mechanics of change usually ensures people handle it poorly.

As managers, such a lack of perceptiveness can lead to inefficiency, loss of production or capital, wasted resources, or even professional disaster.

There appears to be so many different types of change, often all happening at once. Change occurs every day, noticeable and un-noticeable, good, bad, small and large.

Sometimes, our heads spin – too much change for us to grasp and understand – too much to organise successfully.

So how can we cope?

The best way is by understanding how many types of alteration there are and how they work. There are only four kinds of change...

- Pendulum Change

- Paradigm Change

- Incremental Change

- Change by Exception

Every kind of alteration that has ever been will fit into one of those four categories; that fact is as immutable as change itself.

Therefore, understanding what those four categories of change mean, and how they work, will enable us to recognise what type of alteration we are involved in and how best to deal with it.

However, nothing in life is ever simple. Consider another immutable fact…

- There are clearly identifiable natural laws of resistance to change

Conceivably, in the past, you have implemented a straightforward modification – something so easy to understand you ended up wondering why it was not more of an achievement, or even why it failed.

Maybe you assume you found the explanation for why an undemanding alteration did not enjoy success. Perhaps though, you failed to discover the fundamental reason why your simple change did not succeed.

Pendulum Change

Pendulum Change is usually something undesirable. It is a change that does not last. Like the swinging of a pendulum our efforts make an alteration in one direction but maybe, for a plethora of reasons, it is not sustained and the situation returns to the way things were.

Think about this example…

Jack decides to give up smoking. He stops for two or three days, but the nicotine urge is too much and he starts again. It was a completely wasted effort. By the end of the week, he has achieved nothing.

In fact, Jack may have achieved something worse than nothing. Perhaps strolling round like a bear with a sore head, which is a notorious symptom of the first few days of not smoking, might have damaged important relationships or left vital tasks undone.

- Why did the smoker fail?

- Why did his adjustment become a Pendulum Change?

Consider what you have attempted on different occasions. You will begin to see Pendulum Change has touched all of us at some time or another.

We have all swung the pendulum of alteration one-way and it has swung right back at us. Think about this example in the workplace…

Joe produces widgets by hand. He makes fifty a day. His manager decides to make a change, one that will increase the companies' profits and actually makes life easier for Joe.

Nobody should lose. Indeed, everybody stands to gain. The manager buys a machine Joe can operate; it will make one hundred widgets a day. Everything is fine for the first three months. Production doubles, but after six months things are back to the way they were and the machine is standing idle in the corner.

Some reasons will be as individual as the change itself and only relate to that one specific subject. They can soon be identified when you grasp the rationale, for there are repetitive causes for Pendulum Change…

- Lack of planning and research

- Lack of resources

Planning and research are essential to any change. Most plans begin with an idea.

'I think I'll give up smoking, I'll stop from tomorrow.'

Great sentiments, but not much of a plan, no research and little in the way of resources.

- What coping strategies are in place to support the smoker?

- How has he modified routines and habits that promote smoking?

- Does the smoker understand the enormity of the task ahead and how addicted he is?

- What resources are available to assist success?

- Are people near-and-dear aware of the proposed change and ready to supply active support and encouragement?

- Have any anti-smoking aids or expert advice been considered?

Back to the workplace example – Joe and his widgets.

Again, planning, research and resources are necessary if success is to be enjoyed and Pendulum Change avoided.

- A widget-making machine was purchased and apparently, Joe could work it; but could he maintain it?

- Was an ongoing maintenance system of any kind put in place?

- Did the machine come from an established firm with a good record of accomplishment, or were they the cheapest option. Are they now bankrupt, leaving Joe with an obsolete machine and no spare parts?

- Were systems put in place for monitoring the machine's production and performance?

Everything stated so far may seem transparently obvious to many managers, yet it still needs proclaiming because statistics confirm that many undesirable pendulum changes can be traced to a lack of such elementary action.

- No one can make lasting change unless it is well planned, researched, then properly resourced

- False economies usually lead to greater loss when the pendulum swings back

- No change will be lasting if it is not monitored and supported

Something less obvious, is the first of the identifiable natural laws of resistance to change I mentioned earlier.

Natural laws and human instincts are things that exist and evolve because of intrinsic genetics and how the universe exists.

Probably the most well-known human instinct is called fight or flight. That impulse allows us to run away at our best speed or put up resistance, with heightened awareness and physical capacity, when placed under extreme pressure. There are less well known, but similar and just as entrenched, instincts within us resisting nearly any kind of alteration.

Paradigm Change

Paradigm is not a word commonly figuring in most people's vocabulary. However, paradigm is very meaningful; it can be used in place of words such as concept, hypothesis, theory, idea, pattern, matrix, precedent, archetype, model and many others besides.

When linked with the word change though, the meaning of paradigm becomes singular.

Paradigm describes how many changes start. It is the most exciting type of alteration but can be the most hazardous.

So easily, Paradigm Change can become a Pendulum Change. Planning, researching and resourcing are rules that must be rigorously applied to any Paradigm Change.

Paradigm transformation is much more fundamental than, often ill conceived, Pendulum Change. It is the acceptance of a fresh way of thinking, a new set of rules or innovative concepts. Out of the box – colouring outside of the lines – lateral thought – quantum leap, you choose the cliché, they all apply.

- Paradigm Change describes an original idea and the new procedural thinking and practice required to implement the change

Imagine Air travel has just been invented. You live in Penzance and you want to go to New York in the USA. Going to New York is your new idea, your concept, the Paradigm Change to your way of life. However, you cannot get there directly from Penzance or Plymouth, the way you always went. First, you must travel to London Heathrow.

Technically, you are travelling new ground and going further away from New York in order to get there, but doing so is the only way to achieve your goal.

If you apply the equation of a new concept to a less obvious required change, you begin to use a new way of thinking. Suddenly you are planning in a completely new way. Thinking laterally and considering it might be alright to colour outside the lines – preparing for a quantum leap, which will result in a Paradigm Change.

So, you have had your Paradigm mind shift, started thinking differently and are about to make a paradigm alteration. You have planned researched and resourced. What can possibly go wrong and alter paradigm to pendulum?

The answer is people's blind, instinctive, resistance to change – that includes you!

Remember the Pendulum Change concerning the smoker, who gave up, then started again after a few days? He had his idea, but it was not paradigm and it did not have something called visual pay value.

- Everything we do, we do because of visual pay value; that is a natural law and an immutable fact

Getting visual pay value does not mean there is something wrong with us, that we are being selfish or greedy, it is perfectly natural. It means for everything we do there is a reason, no matter how simple or complex, selfish or selfless, conscious or unconscious. That reason has value to our being. Visual pay value.

Quite often, a problem for managers is, the Paradigm Change envisaged has visual pay value for the manager, board of directors and shareholders, but not the workers involved in the alteration.

- Visual pay value provides motivation; but motivation does not always contain visual pay value

Let us go back to the smoker. Arguable his motivation was knowing if he gave up smoking his chance of an early death or possible ill-health would be reduced, but it wasn't visual, it was too hypothetical and in the distant future.

Remember, it is a natural law we are dealing with, something instinctive and unthinking, part of our fundamental being.

The smokers' real visual pay value was how good the nicotine felt. Negative perhaps, but very visual and of great value to him.

Despite some motivation from higher ideals, his paramount visual pay value took over and he went back to his forty-a-day habit, the victim of a Pendulum Change.

It is worth carefully considering exactly what all change is:

- Change is a significant emotional event

- Change is either caused by, and/or results in, a significant emotional event

Understanding and accepting the above important points enables a manager to realise the very powerful forces at work when even a small alteration is contemplated.

If managers appreciate what happens emotionally, as well as all the practical considerations, it makes planning, researching and resourcing take on a completely new dimension.

Incremental Change

Incremental means change over a protracted period; by its very nature, it is less of a significant emotional event.

When altering things, even if starting with a Paradigm idea, long-term Incremental Change should be the target. Of course, an adjustment for a measurable limited period could be the objective, in which case a Pendulum Change would be planned.

Incremental Change is the most successful and lasting change there is because alterations occur slowly, the people involved do not notice so much.

- No one can fully explain why all human beings have an inherent resistance to change

Despite similarities, every human being is a unique individual therefore, some resistance to change is unique as well. However, there is recognisable collective natural resistance to change – one type is called cognitive dissonance.

Cognitive dissonance is a disharmony of thought patterns, which cause us to block many things out and lock on to only one or two familiar, safe and accepted models of events. It can be a part of someone's basic insecurities, prejudice or a whole host of other complex individual emotions.

There is no all-encapsulating explanation for cognitive dissonance other than to say it very obviously exists, has tremendous influence and must always figure in our considerations. The following examples are an expression of cognitive dissonance at work:

Joe Blogs has just purchased another Ford motorcar. As he drives along, he consciously notices nothing but Fords.

'Look dear; there's another one. Good cars Fords, everyone that knows about cars buys one.'

Joe does not mention any other make of car until...

'Look, there's a Nissan, broken down! Should have bought a Ford shouldn't he?'

Buying a new car was a significant emotional event for Joe, his other Ford had lasted ten years. He could not face thinking of another make of car as well as the sale of the old one and the purchase.

Fred is working hard in the garden and being confronted by his wife:

'Have you mended the door lock yet Fred?'

'No but I will when I'm not busy... later.'

Clearly, the door lock is more important than digging the vegetable patch but try telling a perfectly intelligent human being such a thing sometimes.

The digging is harder work, so laziness does not enter the equation. Obstinacy? Hatred of his wife? Possible, but cognitive dissonance is the more likely answer. Perhaps it is better not to try and completely understand cognitive dissonance, simply accept that it exists and be prepared for it if it occurs.

- Do you recognise yourself in similar situations?

How often do we blank out alternatives that have become too many to be comfortable with and lock on to just one? It is a habit virtually everybody suffers from.

- All human beings are creatures of habit

- Insecurities, to a greater or lesser degree, haunt us all; they are a part of our fundamental makeup

Insecurities are hard to live with and can cause us to need constant reassurance for the things we do. We look for supportive reassurance not just from other people but from ourselves as well.

However, by locking out evidence other than that which supports our way of thinking and decision-making, we can often become blind to other viable and perhaps better alternatives.

- Being creatures of habit facilitates systems and basic organisation

Where change is concerned, quite often habits become custom and practice that nobody wants to alter while such practice has visual pay value. How on Earth do we ever get anything done with so many hang-ups?

The simple answer is that human beings are very complex. For every negative there will usually be a positive, finding them when required takes perception, understanding and human empathy.

There are a multitude of other things going on inside our minds as well. Things like determination, desires, curiosity, a thirst for glory and success, plus unique personality facets.

- Human emotions need to be considered by us when we contemplate a change

- Managers making any type of alteration should always study the human factor and how it impacts upon what they want to do

- Events may make a Paradigm Change the only alternative and even patently desirable by everyone involved, but resistance can never be wholly negated

If we go back to Joe and his widgets, it seems his manager needed to increase production and wanted to give Joe an easier working day. So buying a machine that would double production and do most of the work for Joe seemed quite an obvious change. Yet Joe's manager still failed to make his Paradigm Change into a successful incremental one.

- Even simple alterations have inertia, which can often be complex

- Such natural torpor is always a component of change and must be monitored and dealt with

Incremental Change allows people to adjust. From a management point of view, it helps if major Paradigm Change can be broken down into small easily planned and handled parts. Then the incremental process begins immediately.

People involved in a change accept alterations more readily over a prolonged time.

- For Incremental Change to be successful, it needs to be monitored continually and supported during the whole protracted process

- Support needs to be of a remedial nature and consist of actions designed to put the planned change back on track as and when required

- Monitoring should be in audit form with clearly measurable benchmarks

- The more human factor involved, the more support is required to make any change a success

Change by Exception

Change by Exception is an abstract category of change because it has two very different meanings.

The first meaning is exactly that, an exception! Remember there are only three certainties in life; birth, death and change itself. Everything else happening during our existence is a possibility or a probability. Often, both are laced with lots of surprises and exceptions to what we imagine will be.

Changes by Exception are unplanned and are often due to an extraordinary set of circumstances, or exceptional people.

- Incremental Change is long term and lasting, quite often it goes unnoticed

- Paradigm Change occurs because of new dimensions of awareness, bright ideas and new ways of thinking

- Pendulum Change is an alteration that does not last for a plethora of reasons

- Change by Exception is the exception to the other three: an extraordinary change brought about by an unplanned event, circumstance, or action

The natural laws of resistance to change are contained within the other meaning of Change by Exception. When someone makes a personal success of a change we do not want to be a part of, we may well say that person is an exception.

'Jane gave up smoking. Did it without any help too.'

'She's extraordinarily strong willed. I couldn't be like that.'

'Yes, she's an exception.'

By making such excuses to others, but especially ourselves, we can happily live without changing something. Our herd instinct – the majority is the norm – allows us to be right when, in the back of our minds, we know we are wrong.

We excuse ourselves the discomfort of offering any honest explanation by declaring the minority to be an exception.

All of us reside in a personal comfort zone. The zone is created out of habits, experiences, skills, self-image, attitudes, prejudice, fears, preconditioned beliefs and finally, unique negative human emotions, which are probably genetic. All these things are barriers to change.

Examine your own comfort zone. What stopped you from making a change that you know should have been made?

Do any of these quoted clichés sound familiar?

- *'I'm too old to change now.'* [Self-image]

- *'If it's not broken, don't try to fix it.'* [Habits, experiences and skills]

- *'I can't stand him or his ideas.'* [Attitude and prejudice]

- *'You can't sail any further; everyone knows the world is flat.'* [Preconditioned beliefs]

- *'It might not work.'* [Fear]

- *'No! I just couldn't do that.'* [Unique negative human emotions]

For each example given, most people can add at least one other. It is important managers recognise these things within individuals and how they naturally make people resist change.

- Knowing ourselves helps us understand others

It is very easy to mistake the comfort zone for being in a rut, they are not the same.

Being in a rut is usually a matter of life's routines. The comfort zone is far more complex and involves psychological aspects of our being.

Completely understanding the psychological makeup of human beings would probably require more than one lifetime. Recognising and accepting the existence of the human factor as a constant and natural presence that will influence any change is what matters.

There are ways to get people out of their individual comfort zones. Ensuring visual pay value is one of the best. Motivation is another way, though not so effective.

Predictably, similarities between motivation and visual pay value can be found, money is probably the best example. Often, the prime reason for people working, money is a powerful, if somewhat crude, motivator and to some extent satisfies the – what's in it for me? – simplistic fraction of visual pay value.

- By itself, money never ensures dedication or enthusiasm

Negative motivators such as, *'If you don't do that properly, I'll sack you,'* rarely enjoy sustained success.

Negative motivation in all forms is a last resort that fair play, and sometimes desperation dictate, but it has little to do with accomplishment or efficiency.

Most negative motivation is a result of poor management rather than a deliberately obstreperous workforce. There are several ways to positively motivate:

- Be likeable! If people like you as a manager, they will want to do well to please and support you

- Be honest! People support and respect someone they can trust

- Explain career prospects! Often, people respond to long-term motivators such as promotion or condition enhancements

- The security of knowledge makes for a contented workforce

- Self-esteem! Ensure you fully explain how important a job is so people feel they are doing something worthwhile

- Job satisfaction! Although many tasks are repetitive or boring, if a manager ensures they mentally stimulate, job satisfaction can be obtained – pick the right person for the job

A motivated person is more receptive to change. However, managers also need to understand the comfort zone in more depth and see the vast difference between visual pay value and motivation.

Being in a rut means you have become a product of life's routines. There is nothing wrong with life's routines unless you believe there is. You are not a victim of them unless you think so.

Being in a rut, or not, depends entirely on an individual point of view, the personal assessment of oneself and situation. Others may well express opinions, but when considering whether or not you are in a rut, only your decision is relevant.

- Everybody has a comfort zone

We all live within parameters we set for ourselves. Other people with more power set parameters that obviously have influence upon us, but within those social or professional constraints, we set our own limitations and preferences. Parameters that we are comfortable within; those psychological limitations and preferences become our comfort zone.

- The comfort zone is an individual's greatest unconscious resistance to change; it regularly defies sound rationale and common-sense

The unconscious influence of comfort zones is often the hidden reason why so many proposed changes fail. Paradigm Change especially necessitates new ways of thinking. New ways need a person to step out of their comfort zone, to do such a thing, even willingly, requires tremendous mental effort.

We become too uncomfortable emotionally and affected by cognitive dissonance.

- Fears, emotive issues, confrontational situations or self-image

- A mistaken and unsubstantiated belief of more work for no extra recompense

- The threat of re-training

- Preconditioned beliefs and habits

The above points are not incontestable, but everyone you know, including yourself, will have displayed some of them when affected by change.

- Nobody really wants to leave his or her comfort zone

- In order to get people out of their comfort zones, they must be enthused with personal goals – ambitions having clear visual pay value and they must be self-motivated

A Goals and Ambitions Model

Imagine two circles, one within the other; size does not matter, as they are part of a natural dynamic, continually altering.

The small inner circle is our area of influence, the large outer circle our area of concern. No matter what anyone's personal goals and ambitions might be, everyone's unconscious aim is to expand their area of influence and reduce the size of their area of concern.

Anything that affects us arouses concerns within us: curiosities, worries, desires and awareness in general, begin to pester us and continually form the outer circle.

We then attempt to expand our influence so we can control our concerns. The concerns give us visual pay value and the energy to expand our circle of influence.

- The outer circle provides the visual pay value that enthuses us to leave our comfort zone and make change

- The inner circle provides the energy to successfully complete change

Understanding how the human factor influencing change can impact upon plans enables managers to manipulate the procedure and influence outcomes.

Understanding change allows us to achieve more effectively and efficiently. Most importantly, knowing how change affects people allows planning to be optimised realistically.

5

Relationships

Relationships within a professional career are often as complex as a person's private life. Sometimes, it becomes difficult to separate the two. Inevitably, one will affect the other.

Managers' relationships have a more critical effect in both cases.

Personal Relationships

- Never bring your personal problems to work. Managers cannot allow themselves the luxury of such indulgence

- For a manager, sympathy from a collective workforce does not exist, despite the apparent willingness of many staff to empathise with you

The realism of the above statements is controversial, some may think cold and inhuman, or at best cynical. However, collectively, it is the best advice a manager can have where private lives are concerned.

A manager's job is demanding and complex. Relationships with staff are never simple and require concerted effort to manage; they do not need the complications, or vulnerabilities, of personal intimacies becoming public knowledge or rumour.

There is no such thing as a secret, except those unshared and taken to the grave. Share your personal details with a colleague and they are no longer secret, almost certainly, someone else will notice or find out.

- Irrespective of what emotions are cavorting inside, you must control them

- Always exhibit a predictable professional demeanour; if you cannot do that, then you are not fit enough to be at work

Personal relationships within the workplace can be a minefield. Like the new millionaire who suddenly becomes attractive, managers should always wonder about the motivations of anyone expressing a personal interest.

People seeking advancement sometimes lack both scruples and morals. For managers, there is a great deal of opportunity to become the victim of allegations of impropriety. A broken heart can be harder to reason with than the most militant union official and will predictably result in damaging unpleasantness.

Necessary laws that protect human rights, employees in general, and women and minorities in particular can become double-edged swords in the hands of the unscrupulous who seek revenge.

Whenever people spend protracted periods together, personal relationships develop. Therefore, although eminently desirable, it would be naïve to suggest managers should never become personally involved with staff working for them.

If the inevitable happens to you and a personal relationship develops within the workplace, the following suggestions may prove useful.

Set Parameters

- As cold and calculating as it may seem, setting parameters when a private relationship first develops could save public humiliation if things go wrong

- Explore the other person's expectations and explain the vulnerability of your position as a manager

- As gently as possible agree a code of behaviour while in the workplace. If the other person's feelings are genuine, they will concur and understand

Inform Someone

By telling someone else about your relationship, you have an insurance policy if things go wrong – preferably another manager – and make sure the object of your affections knows.

Such action keeps things open. From a positive point of view, it shows commitment. The negative benefit is you have an independent witness to a relationship historically entered into willingly by both parties.

- A witness can provide powerful mitigation and possibly save your career in a worst case scenario

Be Discreet

- Discretion is not just the better part of valour, it is sound common-sense; that should be a manager's greatest attribute

- There are good reasons for discretion in the workplace regarding all personal relationships; some are of vital importance

- A third party might decide to maliciously target your close friend if they want to hurt you

- Never forget why you are at work, you are being paid to serve the needs of the company, not your own desires

How you handle a personal relationship in your professional life speaks volumes about you. It can tell your boss you are stable, a good example, and blessed with the kind of image the company wants to portray.

On the other hand, you could be projecting the attributes that make some directors and senior managers cringe. Either way, discretion can only assist.

Third Party Personal Relationships

Being the arbiter when the professional duties of workers become affected by personal relationships is often an issue faced by managers. There are no winners and no points to score whatever the outcome. Someone usually gets hurt and you might lose at least one good employee.

- It is not unknown for the innocent well-meaning manager to become dragged into a messy situation

- Remember, some mud always sticks no matter who throws it

There are no hard and fast rules to learn when considering how the personal relationships of others should be managed in the workplace. Perhaps it is best not knowing about them at all; ignorance is so often blissful.

However, where relationships are obvious, monitor them carefully and watch for problems. Do not be afraid to let the people concerned know you realise what is happening. If their relationship is obvious, they are unlikely to be offended. A gentle reminder of where they are and the associated pitfalls is often useful.

Professor Abraham O'Dare perhaps gives the best advice for a manager regarding the personal relationships of employees…

'Only get involved in other people's personal relationships when you've no other alternative. And if you've no other alternative? Find one!'

Manager/Worker Relationships

One of the hardest things to do is generalise about relationships between human beings; because people are unique, so is the association between them. Nevertheless, some thoughts on how a manager approaches his workforce are worthwhile.

Remember though, every manager is unique as well, what works for one personality may be anathema for another.

- In the work place, a manager may have many colleagues and acquaintances, but no real friends

- Accept the fact that, although you may want to be liked, often you need to say things staff do not want to hear. Settle for being respected

- Forget servility or aggression; assertiveness and consistency are the attributes a manager should strive to project

- Treat everyone as an individual and respect their individual needs, but treat them all the same

- Your staff may or may not know their limitations. Managers should know everyone's, including their own

- Always be honest, but strive to be diplomatic, remember you are dealing with people who have feelings

- Relationships are rather like a wood fire in a hearth; they both need regular attention and fuel to keep them alive

- Always strive to meet an employee's needs, but make sure they realise that extraordinary favours are two way streets

- Tell your workers how you feel management/staff relationships should exist, then seek their perspective

- Deal with small hiccups in relationships before they have a chance of growing into heartburn

- If the workplace becomes full of bad feelings, there will not be enough room left to do the job

- A positive gesture at Christmas can reap rewards for the rest of the year

A manager should have a conscious feel for relationships in the workplace and the atmosphere they will irrevocably engender. Good relationships breed positive atmospheres, smooth performances and real achievement. A negative atmosphere and poor relationships mean problems.

The Critical Relationship

Within every flourishing organisation, there exists a critical relationship; it is usually abstract and often hard to identify. This association is almost certainly responsible for the major achievement a company enjoys.

If the critical relationship is maximised a business will be completely successful within the obvious financial and material constraints.

- If the critical relationship suffers so does success

A thriving organisation may not realise what their critical relationship is, or even the need for one. Without realising what the critical relationship is, an organisation could be doing everything right because it is obvious practice and their managers are highly competent.

Nonetheless, it is preferable to take time and try to analyse where the critical relationship occurs so it may be nurtured. When a manager attempts to investigate the critical relationship, it is very easy to assume there is more than one.

- There may be a number of important relationships within a company but there is only one critical relationship

- The decisive association that decides between glory and mediocrity or disaster can be very easy to define. Conversely, it can be difficult, or even unbelievable

HM Prison Service

The critical relationship within the Prison Service is one of the easiest to identify; it is the relationship between Officers and Prisoners. If that correlation is maximised, a well-ordered prison is enjoyed. If it goes badly wrong, riots ensue.

It does not matter what decisions senior management make during the day-to-day running of the Service, so long as they do not interfere with that critical relationship between Officers and Prisoners.

History has proved repeatedly that thoughtlessness or enthusiastic inexperience at the top can negatively influence a critical association with devastating results.

The Prison Service is a fine example of a critical relationship at work and what happens when it becomes disregarded or unsupported (see the Lord Wolfe report into the prison disturbances of 1990).

The Disney Organisation

Walt Disney formed a relationship with the public based on a unique product of family entertainment. People in Disney's company were able to analyse the components of that relationship and reproduce them so the organisation still enjoys high achievement; but who is the critical relationship with now?

The above facts seem to suggest the critical relationship is not just a human-to-human bond. Then what is the critical relationship?

- The critical relationship is something only occurring between human beings

- The critical relationship is a reality many people like and wish to maintain. It is also an association capable of changing into a dynamic abstract

What is reality? Is it the way things are? Alternatively, is it the way people believe they are? There is an important difference.

These are arguable facts: When compared to the majority of other developed countries, England has a history of an indifferent climate, the highest taxes in the world, overpriced property, one of the worst health services, a disgraceful record of treatment for its elderly, a below average education system and a gradual erosion of basic freedoms. It is vastly over-crowded. Those are all arguable realities.

Over sixty million people live in England and thousands more are clamouring to get in. The majority think it the greatest place in the world, which is another factual reality; but the realities contradict, so how can they all be right?

Therein lies the secret of realities and critical relationships.

- The same things often mean something dissimilar to different people, and diverse things sometimes mean the same

Managers need to understand that, what makes reality is what the majority believe it to be and it is the same with the critical relationship. It does not matter if the majority are right or not.

The reality is Walt Disney is dead, but the critical relationship between him and the public is still alive.

As long as the company recognises such a situation, and all the factors making the relationship work are in place, then the conflicting realities co-exist.

The critical association between human beings continues as if Mr Disney were alive and well. Reality and truth rarely have much in common, despite what any dictionary states.

- The success of any organisation depends upon one critical relationship between human beings

- Managers should find out what the one critical relationship is within their organisation and then nurture it

- The critical relationship is not based on truth but reality

Perspectives and Prejudices

- Relationships of all kinds are constantly influenced by subconscious bigotry

- All managers have prejudices and they influence perspective

Prejudice need not have anything to do with race or culture. It is a psychological fact that we gravitate towards people we like and away from people we dislike; those are obvious conscious decisions.

However, it is also a psychological fact that we incline towards people who we subconsciously feel are like us, or whom we would wish to be like. Similarly, people we do not want to be like, and things we consider alien to us, subconsciously repulse.

- When managers make decisions, they should try to be aware of how the prejudice, that everyone has, can influence outcomes

- Striving to be aware of what can influence us helps tremendously when we form professional relationships and opinions

- The apparently nice person is rarely all he or she appears and the unfortunate personality is often more of an asset than first realised

Perspectives Are Formed By Two Things

- Life experiences

- Genetic makeup

What happens to us through life affects the way we are; even the strongest and least influenced people are predisposed by experiences.

Genetically, thanks to our parents, we are also, what we are.

The psychologist's jury is still arguing about which one is to blame most of all for what we do. I rather suspect it is about fifty, fifty.

- Managers must remember how narrow individual perspectives can be and how that can influence relationships

- No manager aged thirty-five, or even younger can possible understand how a fifty or sixty year old can feel

- The male manager can have little concept of the physical and emotional experiences that often beset women

- Women mangers have little understanding of what might be going on inside a taciturn man who displays little emotion

Such natural limitations of experience only become a serious disadvantage if managers forget they exist and fail to consider them.

- Everyone has a perspective

- Everyone is prejudiced

- Perspective and prejudice influence relationships

- Every perspective has serious limitations

- Prejudice is often subconscious but must be accepted and considered

- Nobody is perfect, including managers

Because limited perspectives and subconscious prejudice can influence everyone so easily, it is helpful sometimes if a third party monitors a manager's professional relationships.

Rationalisation by a suitable third party is a necessity in cases where serious decisions about people's lives are made. Probably the best opinion any manager can seek is one from an experienced opposite number. Finally, consider the two following points:

- In nearly every case a relationship produces more advantages than disadvantages

- Employees are usually an organisation's biggest ongoing expense and asset, so the investment in staff/management relationships should never be underrated

~

6

Training

Managers are often faced with the conflict of training versus production and the need to make judgments in those areas. Nearly every manager gets the decision wrong at some time or other.

Not ensuring staff are fully equipped to do the job required of them has cost many businesses a small fortune.

How many of these following statements about training are familiar to you?

- We need to strike a balance

- Now is not a good time for that kind of expenditure

- I can't spare the staff for courses

- We'll lose too much production

- I've too much sick absence and holidays to cope with

- Fred or Bert can show them what to do

You can probably add a few more to the list. They are all statements against what many managers see as that perpetual curse called training.

Nevertheless, the most negative manager knows that if even simple tasks are to be completed in a satisfactory manner some kind of training is essential.

When one considers health & safety and other legislation governing employment it is quite obvious some tuition is mandatory.

Countless accident investigations show a lack of training to be responsible for serious injuries. Mistakes that cause lost production can consistently be traced to underdeveloped skills among the workforce. Poor decision-making can frequently be traced to ill-equipped staff of all ranks.

So why do so many managers resist giving staff training?

Why is training so often cancelled, neglected or given a low priority?

There are many answers to those questions, some as individual as the types of jobs themselves, virtually all have psychological connotations. Where human beings are concerned there is never one simple answer. Fortunately, there are some common identifiable reasons for negativity towards training.

Being a manager means you are on the side of the organisation. You either own the firm or are employed to see business is carried out with maximum efficiency and success. You have far more empathy for the company's goals and ambitions than the rest of the workforce usually have. However, such understanding can lead to something negative known as 'company empathy syndrome'.

Consider This Scenario

An organisation's management collectively believe the workforce does not share the empathy, which they possess for their company. To them, the employees are an adversary.

The managers see themselves as the 'good guys' – the clever ones. They see the workforce as less intelligent, of a lower class and only there to obtain money. The organisation is plagued by the unreasonable demands of a strong far-left union.

Often elements of this fictitious scenario are factual in British industry. Having little company empathy does not make the workforce subversive, lazy, or of any less worth.

- Adversarial situations are usually the workers' response to indifferent or unskilled management

The priorities of managers and the workforce are frequently and understandably different. Those differences should be recognised and happily accepted by everyone.

However, quite often ingrained resentments exist within managers. Among such management, training takes a very low priority.

The 'them and us' concept has existed to the detriment of many organisations throughout history. Management orientated 'company empathy syndrome' causes such concepts. Where the 'them and us' situation exists, trust ceases and frequently, left wing unions' gain popularity.

- Remember, the only reason unions exist is that, historically, management did not treat workers properly

Where there are powerful unions, companies repeatedly become bogged down by deliberate awkwardness and extreme procedure. Any likelihood of training the management and workforce in common-sense concepts, which would have them operating as one cohesive unit having mutual respect for each other, are gone.

Consider Another Scenario

You are the senior manager of a lead and silver refinery. You need a production manager. You employ a young man with a first class honours' degree in metallurgy and a college diploma in business management studies.

After a couple of week's induction, with understandably high expectations, you put him to work. Within a month, production has dropped and the shop steward is knocking on your door threatening all sorts of things.

The same scenario again, but this time you promote from within. You select a middle-aged production worker. He is the most experienced and best worker in the refinery. He is bright and articulate. Everyone respects him and seeks his advice. Within a month of him being production manager, quality has dropped and the shop steward is knocking…

In both cases, the two new managers were well qualified, but were they trained specifically for the job you wanted them to do?

- Did either man possess expert technical and people skills?

- With continual regularity, large companies hand out middle management posts in exactly the same cavalier fashion as the above examples

Often good performers at one rank are rewarded with promotion. They then proceed to achieve with mediocrity or even fail abysmally because they receive little or no training for their new post; quite wrongly, senior management frequently decide experience, or newly gained academic qualification, will be enough.

- Many companies promote people to incompetence

- All promotions must include training for a specific post and meaningful probation periods

- University or college qualifications are constantly given more credibility and respect than they deserve

A degree means someone has a reasonable IQ, completes satisfactory course work, is capable of assimilating information and then reproducing it in an exam situation; it does not mean a person has any common sense, practical or people skills.

Many university graduates walk into management posts with little or no training for the actual position for which a firm is employing them.

- Training is the fountain from which the success of any organisation cascades

- People at every grade within an organisation must be properly trained

- The better the training, the better the staff/management relationships

- Training is a management tool for shaping the minds of their staff

- Training is one practical way of showing staff you care about them

- Training must be an on-going mandatory function given constant support by the most senior levels of management

- Training records for every employee must be maintained

- All training should be certificated and comply with a recognised standard

- Training is not an expense; it is a short, medium and long-term investment that consistently reaps high dividends

- Training is the best way of positively ensuring accountability and therefore, quality and performance

Training for the sake of it can be both costly and ineffective. All training must be constantly assessed for its quality and relevance. A week away in an expensive hotel at a seminar can easily turn into several nights 'jolly' when a few bored managers or ground floor workers attempt to recapture their lost teenage years.

If a manager wants to reward staff by sending them on a morale-building sabbatical, great; however, such activities should never be dressed up as meaningful tuition. Frivolity in hotel bars during nights away from home, or even just the disorientation of a journey and a new environment, demeans serious training.

Unless there is absolutely no alternative, courses away from the place of work should always be avoided.

- Wherever possible, all training should be in-house

There are three types of training.

- Theoretical study

- On the job tutoring

- Practical experience

It is theoretical study that gives managers the biggest headache when trying to apply the in-house location. Not every firm has facilities to provide a classroom situation. Some necessary qualifications can only be gained in specialised places such as universities. Yet I suggest in any organisation, some form of in-house theoretical training is imperative.

- Every organisation should have a qualified trainer

Often new employees are shown what to do by someone experienced but with no tutoring qualifications. Such mentoring can become an example of Chinese Whispers and is how valuable on the job training often fails.

When someone unqualified teaches a new colleague, the unskilled person usually shows the newcomer their way of doing things. They habitually miss out procedures they dislike or may not feel are necessary. Subjects like health & safety or quality standards may become costly omissions managers will deeply regret later.

- No matter what size the company, it should include someone who is qualified to train other workers

'On the job' tutoring is arguably the most valuable training anyone can receive. Although not as fashionable as they once were, apprenticeships allow nearly all qualifications to be gained 'on the job'.

Throughout history, apprenticeships produced some of the most skilled and highly qualified people in industry. 'On the job' tutoring is highly focussed and is carried out in the exact environment where skills gained will be put into practice.

- By using a qualified trainer, managers can be sure employees obtain knowledge properly

- Employees can only be held accountable for their performance if they have been properly trained

- Development and planning often go hand in hand with a training department

- A trainer can provide the foundation on which innovation is built

- Trainers endow the staff with confidence and a visible example of management care

- It is cheaper to send one trainer on an external course than the whole workforce

- There are no ranks so high in an organisation that they do not benefit from the skills of a trainer

The practice in many companies is to adopt a fast track system of promotion. Highly motivated clever people who produce fast visible results and success, where previously stagnation has developed, move rapidly through layers of management.

There is nothing basically wrong with such a system; bright minds with fresh ideas are needed in any organisation. However, some fast tracking may also be as a result of political correctness or diversity, such influences can become a fashion, or even an obsession, born of sycophantic political dogma excluding a common-sense balance of old and new.

- There is no substitute for experience

- Highly developed skills in any occupation can only come from experience

- Practice really does make perfect

Experience is probably the best training anyone can receive; it cannot be bought at any price, yet so often managers undervalue it. One drawback with experience, as far as management is concerned is, it is less amenable.

The motivated inexperienced person will always be more agreeable when it comes to new ideas, it is their opportunity to stamp their ownership on something. New employees may not see pitfalls that a more practiced eye observes.

Experienced staff often look down their noses at bright new workers; especially if the fresh person is promoted above them. Training helps to dispel disharmony between experienced and in-experienced staffing situations and philosophies.

Well-trained managers will always seek a balance of all the positive attributes available to their organisation. Well-trained ground floor staff usually realise a new person in a higher position must be bringing a unique skill to the organisation.

- Staff at all levels must feel valued if an organisation is to enjoy success

- Good management and meaningful training make staff feel valued

Some people have a knack for recalling almost anything while others struggle to remember what they did yesterday. No matter how good or bad we are at remembering things, in a classroom situation, the average person never fully grasps more than fifteen percent of what they are shown or told.

We all have likes and dislikes. Often, not all our preferences are wholly apparent, even to ourselves.

The unconscious constantly guides our actions and influences our habit forming. Remember, all human beings are creatures of habit. Managers want to form the professional habits of the workforce. Therefore, constant on-going refresher training is imperative.

The need to repair and update professional practice within an organisation is just as important as the initial training itself, although not always so obvious.

- Handouts should always be issued that summarize training modules

- Training should motivate staff to read handouts and keep them for reference

- Refreshers must be a part of any training programme

- Refresher training forms the pro-company work habits of staff

Informing staff never weakens a manager's position. Knowledge is power, but you are not fighting a war. Good managers empower their staff, but only once those staff are fully equipped.

7

Disciplinary

&

Grievance Procedures

Employment legislation dictates that it is wise for any business to have clear procedures for disciplinary matters and staff grievances. Those procedures should be able to stand up to the scrutiny of the courts, especially employment tribunals.

- Managers should always consider the possible consequences of decision making, especially where discipline and complaints are concerned

- Managers' decisions regularly come under third-party scrutiny

Not only do shareholders, directors and senior management often study what happens in detail, interested third parties can be expected to examine disputes or disciplinary decisions within companies. Employment tribunals, race relations organisations, the Health & Safety Executive and county or small claims courts will probably affect most managers during their career.

The worth of management decisions is often decided by the quality of initial procedures.

- All procedures governing discipline and grievances should be recorded

- Procedures should be agreed with the unions concerned

- Copies of procedures must be available to staff

Although disciplinary matters and grievances are two entirely different things they are inexorably linked. On many occasions one leads to the other. They should be two completely different documents. However, both sets of rules might be in tandem so managers need to be on the lookout for ambiguity or contradiction.

- Always remember nobody can legislate for everything

Occasions will occur when the rulebook does not cover an eventuality; at such times, a manager's judgment must be at its best. Important, sensitive, decisions without documented procedural guidance are always subjective, especially when scrutinised with the benefit of hindsight.

Whilst making pronouncements, there is one overriding rule that should never be broken.

- All decisions must be based entirely on evidence

If there is no evidence and a manager makes a summary decision whilst acting as an adjudicator or investigator, it can only be based on either emotion or bias.

Without evidence, no decision is ever fair other than exoneration.

Evidence

Evidence, like truth, can be highly subjective. Probably the best definition of acceptable evidence is something that can be produced, then recorded and understood by most people.

Evidence must stand up to scrutiny; if it does not, then it is unacceptable.

Management decision making should be based on the law of probability rather than the criminal requirement of beyond reasonable doubt. Probability is the rule guiding cases in employment tribunals and county courts.

- In work place situations, historic documentary evidence is often the most important

Castigating someone who is consistently late can only be effective if a record detailing times and dates is available to identify transgressions. Warnings given verbally for inappropriate behaviour must be recorded in writing.

Written warnings are issued to the transgressor and would be considered more serious. All historically recorded warnings are sound evidence.

- A court of law takes testimonial evidence given under oath very seriously; however, managers should always be a little sceptical

When staff give you their version of events, always consider what their motivations may be. They are not under oath. Even a third party's statement might be dubious.

Work relationships spawn friendships and enmities alike. Truth can become highly subjective, even where the most honourable person is concerned, if personal feelings get in the way.

- Physical evidence is usually sound

Joe Blogs found in possession of six stolen widgets by factory security at the main gate should be enough to find for dismissal. Joe might argue somebody planted the widgets in his lunch box.

However, if there is a notice in the changing rooms advising everyone to, 'Check your bags, clothing etc. – it's your responsibility if found in possession –

perpetrators will be sacked.' Verdict? Bye, bye Joe! And no feasible repercussions.

What if there is not a notice though? Using the law of probability, Joe probably did steal the widgets. Verdict? Bye, bye Joe; but possible repercussions in a tribunal unless, Joe had signed for a written code of required behaviour.

- You must clearly tell staff what the rules are and be able to prove you have

- Unambiguous evidence should be the only deciding factor in any case

- What can't speak, rarely lies

- Seldom are two versions of events the same

- The benefit of the doubt is not only fair but recordable and can be used in evidence at a later date

If we examine disciplinary and grievance procedures in detail, fine points of an obvious relationship between them emerges.

Disciplinary Procedures and Codes of Behaviour

When considering what kind of behaviour will attract disciplinary proceedings, you must first decide answers to the following questions:

- What are the needs of the company?

- Are those needs reasonable?

- Do those needs reflect trends in society?

- What is unacceptable behaviour?

- Is the code of behaviour and disciplinary procedures acceptable to unions?

- Is the company's code of behaviour and disciplinary procedures acceptable to natural justice?

Some organisation's code of behaviour and disciplinary measures are declared unacceptable by unions. Obviously, it is always best if agreement about such procedures can be reached; however, it is not imperative.

The managerial benchmark is acceptability by the courts and employment tribunals. Few unions will go to war over codes they know have legal acceptability and subscribe to natural justice. As a rule, union solicitors examine all company procedures and are the first to point out irregularities.

Fifty years ago, it would have been impossible to stop staff smoking in the workplace unless there were exceptional reasons. Something requiring scrupulous cleanliness might have justified a smoking ban. However, anything else would have been considered unreasonable.

No smoking in the workplace is now considered realistic and, in most cases, legally enforceable. Intransigence against such a rule would be expected to attract disciplinary action at the very least. This policy reflects the trends of society and is completely acceptable in any court.

A company enforcing something out of step with society's trends would need very good reasons for doing so. Society's fashions are all a part of the intangible known as acceptable natural justice.

- What is reasonable today may be unreasonable tomorrow

Fifty years ago a worker could have mistreated his Asian or African colleagues with abuse relating to their colour, religion or culture. Few managers would have raised a serious objection unless it interfered with production. Such actions would now attract disciplinary proceedings within most organisations and would probably result in legal prosecution as well.

A government agency took disciplinary action against a man who loudly abused the name of Osama Bin Laden shortly after the Twin Towers in New York City were destroyed.

The man was charged with a racial offence concerning the incident. Following an internal hearing, he was dismissed. Arguably, the man had breached the letter of the agency's rules. However, the management concerned failed to consider public opinion of the day.

Both the media and an employment tribunal castigated the government agency's managers. Rather sadly, those managers were unable to see that they had been wrong in any way. In the face of public criticism and adverse comments of an Employment Tribunal Chairman, they were implacable.

The agency has one of the best grievance and discipline procedures in Britain. Unfortunately, the people administering those systems are not so praiseworthy. This factual example serves very well to make the following points:

- Law books, codes of conduct, disciplinary procedures and systems for airing complaints contain rules and process, not justice

- Justice can only be in the hearts of human beings, especially those in authority, or it does not exist

As a manager, you will be judged by the kind of justice you administer. The letter of a rule will have scant regard if everyone believes it to be wrong; your decisions are the same. In a democracy, we rule by consent and cooperation.

- Being right and being fair are often two different things

Codes of behaviour should explain what is expected of staff in clear unambiguous language. If something is obviously open to interpretation, then it should not be there in the first place.

Conversely, a catchall clause should exist. Not all unacceptable conduct can be specifically described. Probably the best two catchall charges are:

- It is an offence against the code of behaviour to commit any act that could bring the company into disrepute

- Staff must not commit any act that is reasonably deemed to be inappropriate or offensive

Remember, catchall charges can be highly subjective. Catchalls must never take the place of straightforward obvious statements like: 'It is an offence to steal from the company…'

A code of behaviour should be in the same document as a company's disciplinary procedures. The document should also contain details of an appeals process.

Fair play demands the system should support the assumed victim and the alleged perpetrator. Natural justice supposes innocence until proof of guilt.

- Someone other than an adjudicator should investigate any behaviour likely to incur a formal hearing so that facts may be established independently and without bias

- A formal investigation should be commissioned by a senior manager and terms of reference issued to the investigators

- Interviews should be recorded, one copy of the recording kept for evidence a second copy for the interviewee

- The alleged perpetrator must see all the evidence concerning the case before any hearing

- Reasonable time must be allowed for an alleged perpetrator to prepare a defence and call witnesses

- An alleged perpetrator should be entitled to assistance from a friend or union official but legal representation at an internal disciplinary hearing should not be allowed

- Following a finding of guilt any appeal should be heard by a manager at least one grade above the adjudicator and who has no previous involvement with the case

- Following an investigation, if there is no case to answer, then all paperwork and recordings appertaining to the investigation should be destroyed

- Following a disciplinary hearing, if no finding of guilt is decided, all paperwork and recordings appertaining should be destroyed

Any organisation's disciplinary process should have credibility with the courts and employment tribunals.

The procedure should declare a list of punishments for when a member of staff is found guilty at a disciplinary hearing.

Example

- Official verbal warning *[usually on record for a maximum of two years]*

- Probation period *[for a maximum of one year]*

- Probation period with re-training

- Written warning *[usually in force for a maximum of one year]*

- Final written warning *[usually in force for a maximum of three years]*

- Demotion *[where applicable]*

- Dismissal

- All punishments can be subject to suspension for a period of one year or less

Grievance/Complaint Procedures

Grievance/complaint procedures are an inescapable reality of today's business world. Legislation governing employment demands high degrees of professionalism. Like discipline and behaviour arrangements, systems for making complaints should be documented and issued to all employees.

- What is the difference between a formal grievance and a formal complaint?

Grievance or complaint has caused much confusion in some areas of employment. At least one area of the Civil Service gives mixed definitions. Although both words mean approximately the same thing, when you start attributing rules and procedures to them, they take on diverse connotations.

In the Civil Service, grievance is linked with the word personal and a complaint is viewed as something relating to all matters professional.

Any case should be dealt with on individual merit. If it involves complaints about other people, then it is personal to some degree or another. If it involves complaints about systems or machines, then it is probably impersonal.

Either set of circumstances can affect the emotions of people in different ways.

One set of procedures is all any organisation needs. The system should be applied fairly to everyone, no matter what personal likes or dislikes may be involved.

Complaint procedures need to, unambiguously, inform all staff how the system works while at the same time assuring the vulnerable they will be supported. Procedures should declare at least some of the following:

- All complaints will be treated fairly and discreetly

- Complaints will be resolved informally wherever possible

- Anyone making a complaint will be supported

- Complaints will be resolved, or an investigation will be implemented within one week

- If a complaint is formally investigated, the code of behaviour and disciplinary procedures will apply

- Anyone found making complaints for the purpose of malicious intent or personal gain will be charged with an offence under the disciplinary procedures

- All persons involved in the complaint process will be updated on a weekly basis

Wherever possible, complaints should be dealt with quickly. Informal resolution is best. However, an informal process should be recorded and form the first part of the grievance procedures. It should be the responsibility of the investigating officer to keep everyone involved informed.

- The line manager of the complainant should attempt to establish the facts

- The line manager should recommend informal resolution or formal procedures

- Wherever possible, discuss the issues and encourage people involved to find a satisfactory solution

- The vulnerability of the complainant must always be appreciated, but the rights of the alleged perpetrator must be respected

- The issues of a protracted investigation must be pointed out to all parties concerned in a clear impartial way

- If matters are resolved informally the line manager must still document everything that transpired and keep the record for a period of five years

If a formal investigation begins, the process can take a considerable time. Investigators need to see everyone concerned and record their statements; generally that includes anyone named by the complainant or the alleged perpetrator.

Following the enquiry, an investigator should prepare a written report for the manager who commissioned the investigation.

When numerous people are involved and the matter becomes protracted, damage can occur. Wounds are opened that sometimes never heal. Destructive animosities develop and stress creates a very negative atmosphere.

No matter how hard a manager might try to overcome investigation inertia, it is almost impossible. When matters involve several people, just trying to assemble everybody for a hearing, especially during a summer holiday period, can take months.

Weekly updates are most important in order to dispel negative rumour. Employment legislation suggests, when serious allegations are made, official procedures of some kind must take place.

In my experience, nobody comes away from complaint and disciplinary procedures without being a little wiser and sadder.

~

8

Problem Solving
&
Dealing with Angry People

An inventor once said, 'We only invent things so they can be manufactured in bulk, breakdown soon afterwards, and cause everybody problems until they buy a new one.'
A world renowned industrialist declared, 'There are no problems only people!'

By the same token, Stanley Baldwin once stated in parliament, 'If we had treated the working people of this country properly in the first place, there would be no unions to cause us problems.'

Nonetheless, there are unions, machines that do breakdown, and around any problem can be found at least one human being.

Solving difficulties is part of a manager's job. However, problems can be so diverse it is impossible to cover every eventuality. Troubles tend to come in four categories:

- Problems with an individual

- Problems with more than one person

- Problems with unions or official bodies

- All other Problems

Problems with an Individual

Problems can range from serious disciplinary issues to health problems or other personal issues. Usually when, metaphorically speaking, the problem starts knocking on a manager's door, it has reached a crisis peak, anything before is more a situation than a real problem.

Problems involving an individual often entail frustration that can easily lead to anger. How a manager calms an angry person can decide how easily the problem can be resolved.

Strategies for calming an angry person

A useful working definition of aggression is:

- Any behaviour perceived by another as being deliberately harmful either psychologically or physically

When you attempt to calm an angry person, there are your own personal responses that you must be aware of:

A) Your own response to aggression:

- Fear – control it. There is no record of a manger being murdered by any worker except during a mill riot in the nineteenth century

- The tough guy syndrome – 'I'm as hard as he is, I won't give way! I can stand nose to nose!' That is how to lose control of any situation. Aggression always escalates when met with an uncompromising persona

- Or, 'I can handle this without any help!' Never be afraid to ask for help if things are getting bad

- Your own aggression – 'Aggression? I'll soon show him what aggression is!' You lose control of the situation and even end up in a fight

- Or, 'She's insulted me and she's hurt my pride.' So what? She will probably apologise when she calms down. You are a highly paid professional

B) Stereotypical thoughts about the aggressor:

- The, I know their type attitude – 'He's a typical troublemaker and must be taught a lesson.'

Despite similarities, remember everyone is an individual and you do not know what is happening until you listen. You are not a prophet.

C) Mistaking signs of anger and aggression

- Worry and anxiety can often be mistaken for aggression. Be careful, find out what you're dealing with first

Once you are consciously aware of your response to anger, you can deal with any emotions that may be unhelpful to a situation.

Undoubtedly, the worst response to someone fuming is answering in kind. Therefore, you need to compose yourself before you can begin calming an angry person.

Self-Calming Strategy

- Literally say 'stop' to yourself before you get worked up and angry

- Use breathing to promote relaxation – take a deep breath, then continue breathing slow and deep

- Continue all activity at a slower pace

- Back away slightly – create a little space between you and the aggressor

- Relax your posture – untense, lower shoulders and arms

- Slightly avert your gaze – still look, but not an eye-to-eye glare

- Lower the tone/pitch of your voice and speak slower – it shows you're calm and slow speech usually gets through anger and registers with someone who has stopped listening

- Slow your movements – on a primeval level, it shows there is no threat intended

By following the self-calming strategy, you communicate non-aggression on every level and, more importantly, you relax yourself.

There is one final tip worth remembering when dealing with an angry person: never let them play to the audience.

Human beings respond adversely in groups. Nobody wants to lose face – some start to 'show off' – such individual insecurities haunt us all.

Therefore, if there are other people near when confrontation begins say, 'Follow me!' then turn your back and proceed to the nearest place where you can be alone with the aggressor. They always follow.

The individual wants confrontation and you are the target. However, an angry person will not follow you indefinitely; if you take too long, he or she will become even more frustrated. So do pick the nearest private location.

If possible, the place you take the aggressor should have chairs. Sitting down immediately relaxes a situation. You should sit down automatically and then offer another chair before you say anything else.

If the aggressor refuses to sit, say nothing. Let the person get whatever is causing the problem off his or her chest; just listen.

When the aggressor finally runs out of steam, ask them to sit down again. In all probability, he or she will comply. Now the problem solving can begin.

Problems with More than One Person

Problems with more than one person really fall into two categories: they have problems with you, (in which case it will probably become a problem with a union situation) or they have problems with each other/others:

- Never negotiate with unofficial groups of staff

- Separate problematic staff and see them on an individual basis

- After seeing staff as individuals you should see them together to feedback a solution/decision

If, for example, three people have problems with each other, speak with them individually and reach a solution, but then speak to them as a group repeating all the main points.

By following this procedure all three people will assume there are no secrets or hidden agendas. You have seen them as individuals, paid attention to their individual needs, but treated them fairly and exactly the same.

- Group problems require group solutions

Problems with Unions

Unions can provide the most serious and potentially damaging problems any manager can face. How you treat staff as individuals will decide how much power the, often lemming like, communal force of the union has.

Sometimes, a union's headquarters have a potentially damaging national agenda, which most of your local workers may disregard – if they are content.

- Solve problems while they're molehills; if they grow to mountains they may become unconquerable

Treat union officials with respect; get them in on the metaphoric ground floor with any proposed change: ask for their opinions and help. They might offer only the obvious; however, such courtesy costs you nothing.

On the other hand, the union might just give you the solution to a problem: never allow stupid pride or snobbish obstinacy to cloud diagnostic good judgement.

- Be an analytical professional, not an emotional amateur

No matter how good a manager you may be, sometimes confrontation with a union is unavoidable.

Benjamin Franklin declared, 'It only takes one rotten apple to infect a whole barrel of fruit.'

On such an occasion, problem solving must always be considered to the worse consequential extreme:

- How will it look to an independent third party?

- How will it look in the newspapers?

- What will be the long-term effects on the company?

Major confrontation should always be avoided by continually monitoring potential situations and dealing with them quickly and fairly before a union has time to think and respond in a damaging way. The complicated answer is, do not implement anything that will not stand up to public and historic scrutiny.

If you ever find yourself in serious confrontation with a union, it is probable that intransigence on both sides will have developed.

Common sense problem solving is often replaced by political point scoring and emotive thinking. At such times, usually, only the arbitration of a third party will resolve issues expeditiously.

Allowing time to pass may eventually wear union members down when monetary concerns begin to bite, but frequently the damage done to a company is even more profound, albeit not so obvious to the public eye.

- Any problems where unions are concerned need to be solved quickly

- Be open, honest and fair

- Never allow personality to get in the way of solution

- Remember the words of Stanley Baldwin

All Other Problems

The last of the four headings also suggests a personal formula for dealing with all problems:

- There are millions of problems every day, all caused by human beings

- Problems will still be there the day you die and long after

- Managers need to continually maintain a sense of proportion

Doctors say prevention is better than cure; so it is with problems. Whenever possible never do anything unless it has been thoroughly researched, well planned, then implemented with the proper support and resources.

Do not take the cheapest option for budget's sake alone because it rarely ends up that way.

Buying plant and equipment must always be underpinned by the credibility of the supplier, guaranteed good performance of the commodity, reliable maintenance and long-term spare availability.

The same equation applies to any other service you contract in as well.

When dealing with people, do not give the more verbose or unreasonable priority over the amenable and flexible, all that achieves is ensuring everyone becomes unreasonable eventually.

- Don't put things off

- Try to visualise the potential of any small matter

- Deal with problems in a systematic, even-handed, visible and professional manner

Fashion, legislation and time have ways of making the unacceptable acceptable. Those intangibles can make yesterday's culture illegal and show problems to be nothing more than a constant reminder of the imperfections of us all.

Finally, remember not to lose your sense of humour, any big problem today becomes tomorrow's unbelievable tall story.

9

Stress

Managers rarely get through their working lives without suffering one way or another from stress. It is an illness that waits, like a killer virus, for our immune system to weaken. Unlike a virus though, stress does not respond to antibiotics and it does not attract sympathy like a large dose of influenza.

Akin to many diseases of the mind, stress is often minimized, or even scorned, yet if it assails you, the effects can be devastating. So what exactly is stress?

- Stress is a response to experiencing demands that are greater than your personal capacities and resources

- A response to stress is a personal reaction involving your body, thinking, feelings and behaviour

When the human body responds to stress, there are two phases, the unconscious, or primary, and the conscious or secondary.

With most bodily functions, unconscious actions are usually involuntary and conscious actions voluntary. However, the response where stress is concerned is common to everyone and there is nothing voluntary about either phase.

The unconscious, as the primary name implies, usually starts first and this is what happens:

- Heart rate and blood pressure go up

- Breathing quickens

- Sugar is released from the liver

- The digestive system shuts down

- Blood clots more readily

- A slight rise in body temperature occurs

- Sweating increases

The conscious or secondary response has three distinct stages. They can occur quickly or over a protracted period depending on the level of stress concerned and the individual involved.

Stage 1

You physically and mentally mobilise to meet challenges. If the stress continues...

Stage 2

Your energy is consumed. If the stress continues...

Stage3

Your energy becomes exhausted and eventually you reach... BURNOUT!

Before burnout is reached, stress will influence the thinking, feelings, behaviour and body. Everyone will experience some of the detriments listed below:

Thinking

- Loss of concentration

- Loss of memory

- Indecision

- Difficulty in 'switching off'

- Difficulty trying to plan

- Ignoring new information

Feelings

- Low and powerless

- Irritable and resentful

- No confidence

- Difficulty feeling any pleasure, joy or affection

- Anxious or even tearful

Behaviour

- Withdrawn

- Lateness or 'going sick'

- No enthusiasm for anything

- Sleeping problems

- Lowered persistence

- Edginess accompanied by snapping and outbursts of temper

The Body

- Headaches

- Chest pains

- Stomach upsets and indigestion

- Cramps

- Extreme tiredness

- Lower resistance to infection

- Lower sex drive

How and when stress affects a person will depend entirely on individual makeup. Some people seem immune to stress and then something small and seemingly insignificant may have a devastating effect.

- Everyone is different

- Stress is a question of balance

Imagine a child's seesaw. At one end are the demands being made upon you, at the other end are your capacities and resources.

All the time the seesaw is exactly horizontal the balance is maintained. You are able to deal with the demands made upon you. Job satisfaction is enjoyed.

Life in general is great. If the balance is upset and demands start to out-weigh your capacities and resources stress begins. Suddenly you can't cope, among other things, 'bang' goes the job satisfaction.

The opposite, out of balance, example of the 'seesaw' illustration is, if your capacities and resources outweigh the demands placed upon you by any noticeable degree, you become bored.

Boredom can be debilitating, but since I've yet to discover a manager who couldn't find more than enough to keep occupied during any given working day, I won't bother describing any coping strategies for it.

Sooner or later, what will be needed are everyday ways of handling stress, so here they are:

- Recognise that problems rarely go away

You can always try the ostrich strategy of metaphorically sticking your head in the sand and hoping for the best, but what you might see is your career being buried in an even deeper hole.

There is a school of thought that states, 'Sometimes, the most brilliant thing you can do is nothing.' I am sure on rare occasions that may be true. However, I've already said, problems rarely go away by themselves, so more proactive tactics are required.

- Managers must work constructively to increase their personal resources

Health is probably any human beings' greatest resource. The healthier you are the more resilient to any debilitation you are. A manager should ensure health as far as possible with a systematic approach that is achievable:

- Take regular exercise

- Maintain a healthy diet

- Get adequate sleep

- Find time for varied leisure

- Take at least one fourteen-day holiday a year

- Have a health check every year

Resources can be increased by physically developing coping tactics that involve others.

Fellow managers or members of your workforce should be involved in developing a support network that provides opportunities for:

- Talking about concerns and feelings regarding the job

- Ways of finding areas of common ground

- Helping others

- Humour

Personal resources are often increased with the assistance of others; problem sharing really can often be problem halving. A manager's capacity to cope may be increased if a problem-solving attitude is adopted at the first signs of stress.

- Don't jump to conclusions – don't be hasty

- Take a metaphoric step back and think

- Accept what can't be controlled, concentrate on what can

- Remember nobody is perfect – not even you

After adopting a problem solving attitude the capacity to cope can be further increased by the use of techniques such as:

- Analysing the problems

- Thinking of possible solutions

- Thinking of consequences

- Making constructive plans

- Rethinking if necessary

Not just capacities and resources need to be worked on. Remember the other end of the seesaw? Managers must be prepared to do something about the demands placed upon them.

Nobody wants a manager who starts moaning whenever big problems or demands arise. However, managers owe a duty of care to their workforce and themselves, they must say when targets are unrealistic or demands are too great.

If ever you decide to voice objections, be sure your arguments are evidential and you have proof close at hand; it is almost certain you will be disagreeing with a senior.

Too many sycophantic managers drive themselves into early graves. Those type of people set ridiculously unrealistic standards that become a rod for the backs of others as well as their own.

Do be prepared to stand up and be counted now and then, such seemingly confrontational action can earn respect and save a heap of protracted stress. Just be sure you are right. Always ensure your perspectives are realistic. Also, consider other ways of working with demands.

Manage Time the Most Efficient and Effective Way:

- Don't put problems off – they only build up

- Break tasks down into manageable steps or stages

- Always work out priorities when multi-tasked

- Strive to be proactive – plan ahead whenever you can

- Make use of accountable delegation whenever possible

Regulate Demands:

- Take scheduled breaks – you need lunch

- Behave assertively – negotiate workloads where possible

- Delegate whenever you can, as a matter of expected practice

- Avoid too many changes at once

- Be prepared to learn new skills

Having worked on your personal resources, capacities and the demands placed upon you, it is important you combine such actions with an attempt to relax when faced with situations that start to cause stress.

- Take a deep breath and then continue to breath slowly and deeply

- Count to ten under your breath – or out loud if you're alone

- Relax your muscles – they're sure to be as tense as the rest of you

If all else fails, utter a profanity under your breath and smile! Remember, you have only one life and heart attacks tend to shorten it considerably!

10

Boardroom Morals

Some managers may not attend meetings where they are vying for a director's attention. Others may not have business rivals that sit around the 'long table' offering smiles and insincere sympathy if they perceive you have a weakness.

If the boardroom never concerns you, disregarding this chapter is still not advisable. All managers need a paradigm perspective now and then.

Dustmen, bus and train drivers, either like each other, or they do not. Such people rarely complicate the working day with the politics of point scoring or advancement. Even the cunning or obsequious among them seldom use their dubious talents as they pursue their occupation.

The reasons why the world of management and the boardroom are so different may at first appear obvious. For a manager, life is far less simplistic. Complex issues and multifarious decisions often require intricate machinations. Delicate issues need careful negotiation if they are to be resolved with any degree of success.

- Ambitions are more acute?

- Careers must be plotted with care?

- Managers have more responsibility?

- There must be politics?

It has been proven in many surveys over the last five decades that the only people who really enjoy politics are politicians.

Managers do not have more responsibility than a bus or train driver. How many people will a manager injure or kill if he makes a serious mistake? What about the bus driver?

- Power corrupts – total power corrupts totally?

Examine power. Managers are powerful people: they can make things happen, hire and fire, maybe cause a large firm to succeed or fail. They decide how hefty sums of money and other resources are used.

A manager can make serious decisions that have a tremendous effect on many people's lives.

Bus and train drivers have the power to kill dozens of people. One wrong decision and not just production suffers; those drivers can do a whole lot more than dismiss people. So who is the most powerful?

Well, it all rather depends upon your outlook and values, but I would suggest the power of life and death is the ultimate power. Based on that argument, a manager is less powerful than a bus driver.

Are managers more intelligent?

Perhaps they are, but if so, how did a taxi driver beat four managers, two schoolteachers and two company directors in a national Master Mind championship?

Perhaps the taxi driver was an exception, [see the chapter about change] though I doubt it. Any intelligence differences are small and irrelevant; it is more a question of ambition.

- Power does not corrupt and total power does not corrupt totally.

What really corrupts is cupidity – the opportunity to gain all the good things in life and to lord it over one's fellow human beings. Those things turn some perfectly decent people into Machiavellian, sycophantic, politically thinking 'slime balls'!

The power numerous professions can wield is far greater than that of managers. The responsibilities others have are more demanding and acute in many occupations.

What makes countless managers power hungry politicians who would stab their own mother in the back for another promotion is the type of person the job attracts and, more importantly, the environment in which they find themselves.

In numerous cases, where there exists a command or lengthy management structure, people count themselves failures if they do not eventually claw their way to the top. Many junior managers even set goals to reach by a certain age and heap tremendous stress upon themselves accordingly.

- If countless managers cared as much about their current job as they do about their next promotion, the quality of their work would go up considerably

- The insecurities, resentments and naked ambitions haunting the management profession are far greater than in any other field of endeavour, except politics

To analyse and understand the reasons why much of management is amoral and damagingly competitive would take a couple of life times. Raison d'être suggests such a diverse spectrum as class snobbery to inferiority complexes and a lack of visible creative talent.

None of the main reasons discovered, in any in-depth surveys, have ever been particularly complimentary when attempting to establish why people become managers.

The rules of the boardroom:

- Never entirely trust anyone

- Never completely trust anything anyone says, unless in writing and signed, even then, remember all things are subject to change

- Beware of professional hostility; be even more aware of professional friendship

- If you have an idea send a copy to all the other managers, that way no one can secretly steal it

- Always be polite, skulduggery has etiquette

- Try not to be the first to leave meetings and try not to be late for them, unless you want the other managers to talk about you

- Metaphorically, sing only from the company hymn sheet unless asked to join the choir

- Keep your briefcase locked and make sure you have the only keys to your desk draws

- Remember you've got to live with yourself

- Ambition is commendable, so is dedication, but professional aspirations are cold comfort when the lights go out

- Success comes at a price, be sure you can afford it

- Boardrooms are like the Southern Ocean; on a good day most attractive, but trying to survive a storm in either can be hell

Vocation and ambition are alive and well in other professions besides management and politics [politicians are allegedly managers and supposedly manage countries].

Stereotyping is something always to be avoided. Nevertheless, it is hard to find any other occupation so in need of a moral spring-cleaning.

- It is a fact, management in Great Britain is among the worst in the developed world

Caring about what we do and the people who work for us [examine the Japanese model of management practice] is just as important as caring about production, achievement and ambition. Like many things in life, it is a question of balance.

~

11

Delegation and Teambuilding

Delegation and teambuilding can be more rewarding than many other areas of managerial work. Delegation allows good professional relationships to develop. Teambuilding allows visible group achievement to be realised.

Professor Rensus Lickart, an eminent psychologist, stated, 'Managers should delegate work to the lowest level possible because that's where the majority of the workers are.'

However, perhaps a note of caution needs to be expressed. My particular favourite in the field of psychology, Professor Abraham O'Dare, once remarked, 'The harder someone works the more they get taken for granted. Human nature requires one to always whip the willing horse.'

- How many managers' actions reflect either of those statements?

Delegating and Prioritising:

Professor Lickart is correct. One man can never do the work of six and six cannot do the tasks of ninety. You would be amazed how many managers unthinkingly subscribe to that type of equation though. It is as if, by passing on a workload, those in charge would be letting the level of workers below know something they should not.

Some senior managers would rather run themselves ragged doing extra tasks than give away, what they perceive to be, power.

Winston Churchill remarked that, 'Knowledge is power.' However, I feel quite sure old Winston did not contemplate doing much of the manual work himself!

- It's only insecurity that stops delegation

- Remember that delegation is not abdication

Someone once asked the managing director of a very successful engineering company what tasks he completed. He replied, 'I don't do anything specifically, I get everyone else to do all the work, but I poke my nose into everything.'

Those words sum up the art of delegation, keeping your finger on the pulse while the work is done around you. Remember what a manager is – a facilitator, nothing more nothing less.

- Facilitating is a supportive role

- Support isn't always about solving other people's problems

- Delegation means having time to make decisions

- Delegation requires having faith in staff to carry out the tasks that they have been well trained to complete

- Be sure you equip staff before you empower them

That last statement hints at why many managers suffer from one particular aspect of insecurity. I cannot overemphasize the importance of good training. Sadly, some managers secretly have little faith in their company's levels of tuition or systems of working.

This is what real management is all about; tackling big issues such as ensuring training and systems are right so that delegation is both practical and obvious.

Never find fault for the sake of it, but be mature and honest enough to put the long-term interest of the company first. Identify poor practice and have a constructive plan for improvement at the ready.

- Making visible decisions is authentic management that aids delegation

- Think, gather evidence and produce common sense plans

- Staff willingly accept responsibility when working from the foundation of confidence provided by a manager's supportive common-sense example

- Facilitating is solving problems so that things run smoothly

- Delegation means solving problems by encouraging others to solve problems

The difference between delegation and management abdication has nothing to do with work loading. Encouraging others to solve problems is not abdication. Abdication is when you do not even know there is a problem.

Many managers quite like the way their junior supervisors bring them dilemmas. Perhaps the parental instinct haunts many a senior boss. All it really means is a junior supervisor has succeeded in solving his or her problem.

By passing a quandary upwards, it ceases to be a junior's problem – delegation in reverse to be exact. Obviously, there are some predicaments that junior managers are not equipped to solve. However, letting them pass their dilemmas up the chain of command ad-infinitum is not a satisfactory solution either.

- Keep junior members of staff involved

- Give hints, but expect juniors to provide suggestions

- Guide juniors to find their own solutions

Problem solving can become a useful training medium if tackled in the right way. The rather sycophantic buzz statement – 'there are no problems only opportunities' – frankly makes me cringe.

Nevertheless, it is a manager's job to make the best out of any situation and if something negative can become a practical learning opportunity, so much the better.

- Delegation doesn't mean losing power, but it does mean sharing some, that's something many managers are uncomfortable about

- A senior manager either is, or is not, in charge; allowing someone else the authority to make decisions doesn't alter seniority

- Giving someone else power only enhances your own; the key factors are responsibility and accountability – delegation, not abdication

- Encourage junior grades to suggest solutions to problems; it provides experience and experience is the greatest teacher in the world

- A senior manager must set parameters and ensure accountability

By making junior managers understand that having authority means they are responsible and accountable for what they do, the senior's authority remains undisputable. The same equation applies right the way down to the lowest grades.

Just as Rensus Lickart advises, the more work passed down the grades, the more efficiently tasks are completed – simple arithmetic.

- Delegation requires careful prioritisation

- Delegation is about empowering people who have been equipped

- Many hands make light work

- Delegation means more time to see someone else is working properly

All work should be prioritised. In many cases, priorities are obvious... 'The widgets must be ready by Thursday, but the ospods aren't needed until Saturday.'

Most staff will immediately realise that the widgets must be produced first. The staff will know, that is, if somebody tells them.

When managers delegate they must be very clear about exactly what they want in their own minds first.

Often junior staff are wrongly castigated because simple jobs fail to meet expectations. Investigations frequently show tasks being communicated without any priorities.

By the time senior managers get around to delegating, they usually have a complete picture. Unfortunately, 'knowledge is power' often kicks in and natural human instinct makes it feel uncomfortable when sharing information.

It is no use delegating if the complete picture is not passed down.

- It bears reiteration; managers must equip staff properly before they empower them

- Knowledge might be power but it capitulates to rank and authority

- Prioritising as a matter of routine becomes a system accepted and understood by everyone

To whom should a manager delegate work?

The simple answer is the person most suitable to complete the task.

Remember the words of Professor O'Dare though; 'The harder someone works the more they get taken for granted.'

Again, it comes down to priorities. There are times when only the best staff will do, but if others are good enough to employ, then they are good enough to utilise. Continually using just the best and most willing – or worst still the favourites – causes more problems than any sane manager would ever want. Resentment jealousy, poor team relationships, loss of respect, apathy...

- Don't deliberately delegate work to only certain members of staff because it makes life easier for you – that's a short-term fix leading to long-term problems

Self-Priorities

Personal prioritising is a worthwhile practice that should become habitual. When seemingly endless files, folders or other communications arrive on a manager's desk he or she should always start dealing with the workload by prioritising:

- What needs instant attention?

- What can wait for a few days?

- What can be delegated and in which order?

- What can be filed in the bin?

Such simple systems can be an aid to completing large workloads efficiently. Prioritising aids delegation.

Do not forget to keep records though. Nobody remembers everything. When you delegate, do it in a structured way. Record who you give a piece of work to and 'time bound' it. Check the record regularly and chase anyone not keeping to the set schedule.

By using such a structure, you make a statement about the standards required.

Teambuilding

Ownership is one of the biggest motivators any worker can have. Feeling ownership of the task being performed, or ideally the whole job of work, brings out the best in people.

- Part of the 'ownership' feeling is a sense of belonging to a successful team

Professional relationships develop to a high standard within a well-organised team. Performance and achievement are maximised. Staff enjoy coming to work.

So how do managers achieve such a business utopia?

As usual, there are no simple answers. Teams consist of human beings with foibles, frailties and abilities.

However, when building a team, there are some simple rules to follow that will help produce good results:

- A manager must be sure of exactly what the group is required to achieve and shape a team accordingly

It is no use constructing a team before you know exactly what the task is – a carpenter will not be any use if the job is constructing a car engine – it sounds obvious, but you would be amazed how many managers do not adhere to such a common sense rule.

Tom gets his mate Jack on the group because they play golf at the weekends. Jack then suggests Bob because he's just started playing and always stands his round in the clubhouse afterwards. Tom agrees because he likes a free pint now and then. They all agree on Sally being a member because she's the prettiest girl in the department with the biggest…

Do you recognise anything? Friendships and favourites have a place, that is human nature and it would be dishonest to deny it, but professionalism must always take priority.

Never let relationships, or worse still, base emotions, get in the way of professional common sense!

- Balance is the objective – a balance of personalities, skills and performance levels

A balanced team will always produce the best results. If everyone is a dynamic optimist, things will be done quickly but littered with mistakes. If all the team members are pessimistic, questioning the validity of everything, there will be no mistakes but very little of anything else.

- Remember you are not perfect; try to recruit people with a view to covering your weaknesses and faults

Balance is everything; metaphorically, some people should say, 'the bottle is half full.'

Some should say, 'the bottle is half empty,' and some should say, 'we've got half a bottle!'

- Consider personalities; while it must never be the overriding factor, everyone should be capable of working together without a negative atmosphere

- Think about your authority; although someone may be brilliant if he or she is continually disruptive, leave them off the team

- Consider delegation; there will be times when you're not available, be sure to appoint someone to lead the team in your absence

Team Briefings

Nothing is more important, or obvious, than telling the team, what you want them to do. What is not always so apparent to many managers is telling the team why you want them to do something.

Ownership and motivation can be stimulated more from knowing 'why' something is being done than anything else. 'Why' usually describes the greater goal or long-term vision; it often makes a seemingly unnecessary piece of work make sense.

Knowing why we do things is fundamental to everything we do in our personal lives, why should our professional lives be any different?

- Team briefings should include individual tasking

A team always works better when there are no secrets, real or perceived.

If an individual private briefing is required, then the task has no business with any team, or team member. A manager should allow plenty of time for questions and feedback from team members. You want the team to function as a unit, but they are still individuals.

Questions must be encouraged and feedback should be demanded; such requirements are more acute where teams are concerned. Some people have a natural aversion to asking questions in front of other people; those barriers must be broken down.

Everyone must enjoy complete understanding and the manager's job is to make sure they do. 'Chinese whispers' later between two or three team members is not the way information should ever be communicated.

Plagiarising and Credit

I have seen a manager receive a document containing a good idea from a member of his staff, copy it, put his own name on the bottom then send it to his manager.

I have even known managers who were stupid enough to try taking the credit for what their team had conceived and produced.

- Sycophantic ambition is invariably blind

Senior management do not want juniors who only produce good ideas. Senior management want supervisors who are capable of getting good ideas from other people then displaying the good sense to use them.

Always give credit when someone suggests an initiative. Whether ideas are used or not, the effort of thinking them up deserves some credit.

If someone's plan is adopted, give full recognition when reporting the innovation to a senior. The fact that you are in charge of a team making good progress reflects more positively on your management skills than just having an idea yourself.

- Discuss ideas with the whole team – several brains are always better than one

- Open plagiarism accompanied by honest credit is acceptable

- Amendments are usually better than original statements

- Ensure every team member contributes

- Both good and bad team morale is an infectious disease

- Remember trust is a two-way thing – don't expect it if you don't give it

- Own your team the way you want them to own their job

- Even if the team get it wrong, whenever possible, defend them to others; discipline and remonstrations should be your private prerogative

12

Last Thoughts

The little things matter. One of the best pieces of advice I can give is always think about, and take care of, the little things; if you manage to do that chances are, the big things will not happen.

Time Keeping

Systems for clocking in and out are great; they provide an instant record and require a deliberate and sackable act to subvert.

Shift work is difficult to control without some kind of clocking system. Day work is slightly different, but some kind of written record of attendance must be maintained.

No matter what hours are worked, or how small the labour force, an historic record settles the most virulent disputes.

- Line managers should come to work at the same time, or even just before their staff

I can imagine groans at that proposition. Perhaps followed by statements, 'I've worked hard to get where I am; I'm not keeping those kind of hours now. My time's nine o' clock; I'm not coming in at seven.'

Management is about setting standards. Do not expect staff to arrive and work from a minute past seven if the supervisor does not wander in until half past eight.

Unless staff are subject to a very tight piece-rate pay scheme, the first thing they will probably do at seven is put the kettle on!

The incentive to become a manager should never be about keeping different hours; at least not until director level is reached.

Managers must set examples and be there to manage, if the workforce can cope without you for the first two hours of a day why not all the time? The company could save thousands!

- There are many jobs but few vocations, many workers, but few vocationists

- Remember human nature; everyone loves something for nothing

- Everyone succumbs to temptation one way or another

- Most workers would rather be somewhere other than at work

Pay schemes

Many company's remuneration systems have been arrived at by protracted negotiations usually dating back to the dawn of the firm itself. Typically, they evolve via a history of compromise.

However, occasionally managers get the opportunity to influence pay systems so it is worth considering what types of structure would be best for your organisation. Think about incentives such as possible bonus schemes.

If you produce items in large quantities, then perhaps, a piece-rate scheme is best; unfortunately, there are setbacks to that system:

- What rules will apply if you run out of parts or a machine brakes down?

- Quality can be sacrificed to quantity and needs constant checking

- Continual quota negotiations

- Production governed by machine pace

- Production misappropriation

Nonetheless, piece rate systems do create tremendous incentives when linked to repetitive soul-destroying tasks and they do result in high yield production. Such systems usually include critical union negotiations and need 'tying up' beyond even the slightest ambiguities.

Many companies pay staff on a monthly basis, but there are still a few who pay weekly. Any organisation paying weekly wages that employs people in double figures should attempt the move to a monthly scheme; financial savings are considerable.

Even the smallest firm can make savings if they move to a system of direct payment into bank accounts rather than pay packets containing cash. Financial incentives, like a one-off bonus for moving to such systems, are worth paying.

- What about performance related pay?

An incentive like performance related pay is perhaps worth considering, but it does not come cheap and has a multiplicity of problem areas.

Positive aspects are obvious, the opportunity to reward quality work, increased productivity, good attendance and loyalty; plus there is the opportunity to divide and rule.

However, problems start with, 'Who decides who deserves what?' And continue with, 'What work qualifies and what work doesn't and how is it quantified?'

An annual reporting system is required that provides an evidential assessment of each employee who qualifies for performance payments. It must be a reporting system devoid of subjectivity and capable of standing up to independent third party scrutiny; in forty years I have yet to see one that does. Managers carrying out the reporting process need to be trained and the whole procedure is very time consuming. Human frailties cause allegations of favouritism, vindictiveness and a general lack of managerial observation every payment anniversary.

- What about profit and quality shares?

Profit share bonuses are something that can be given to an organisation's employees with few problems and maximum long-term incentive. Rather like a shareholder's dividend, bonuses depend entirely on the success of the company.

The only negative areas are union negotiations about how much is paid and individual grumbles such as, 'I worked harder than she did, I should have more.' However, profit shares are better than performance related pay.

Although managers should always be on the lookout for ways to save money and improve pay systems, maybe their biggest task in those areas is to spot disincentives.

Some jobs are salaried to cover extensive sickness on full pay. Self-certification usually covers over a week if days off are included. Put the two together and the unscrupulous have a license to take at least one week extra holiday every year and possibly more at no loss whatsoever.

Various companies use a points system to combat sickness abuse. Points are awarded for each period of sickness, after so many points and warnings the abuser can be dismissed. The trouble with such systems is they scarcely differentiate between the abusers and the genuine and are usually controversial and subjective. Such systems are, by necessity, protracted and unproductive.

The best way to combat sickness and absenteeism is an attendance bonus. Strive to control annual pay awards vigorously, but be far more flexible where an attendance allowance is concerned. The company ends up paying a large yearly, or monthly, bonus; but if cost of the bonus is offset against pay awards, accumulative interest might make the firm's accountant smile.

- Professor O'Dare stated, 'Overtime rates and attendance bonuses have cured more sickness than penicillin'

Undermining

Being undermined by higher authority must be one of the worst things that can happen to a junior manager. Some insecure or sadistic senior managers seem to delight in such actions.

Other common reasons for seniors undermining juniors are thoughtlessness, a simple lack of diplomatic procedure, or even a genuine desire to be of help. If you have supervisory staff working for you, remember their feelings and the importance of their credibility.

If a junior manager makes a wrong decision, unless it is imperative to act immediately, do not alter it. See the person concerned privately and tell him or her to change the situation. That way the junior manager learns a valuable lesson about the responsibility of decision-making.

Importantly, he or she does not lose face. With words to the staff [affected by the poor decision] like, 'I think I might have been wrong about that and I'm going to alter my decision...' a junior not only has the liability for correcting his or her own error but, by admitting a mistake and being willing to change, the manager shows considerable character and gains respect.

Be aware of the deliberate or unconscious undermining committed by members of the workforce as well. There are many reasons why some staff will seek to ignore their line manager and go to someone more senior:

- A perception that the line manager does not have enough authority

- A perception that seniors dislike the line manager

- Too close a relationship to be impersonal

- Dislike and a lack of respect

- A desire to undermine

- Secrecy

- A complaint about the line manager

Unless it is a serious complaint against someone where obvious confidentiality is required, a line manager should always be informed of any application from a worker to a senior.

If a member of staff wishes to speak with a senior manager, in most circumstances, such a request should be granted. Even if the senior manager could deal with the problem very easily, unless it is impossible for the line manager to resolve the issue, the senior should always refer the member of staff concerned back to their supervisor. Sound reasons exist for doing this:

- A desire not to undermine

- A wish not to end up with more problems than necessary

- Visually supporting the line manager

- Sending out a signal that the line manager has authority and support to solve problems

Employing Staff

While on the subject of support and credibility, it is worth looking at how companies employ staff. Some advertise, others use a local employment office and some do both.

Large organisations usually leave recruitment to personnel or administrative [admin] departments; this can cause problems.

Quite often, admin departments have little knowledge of the jobs for which they are recruiting people. No matter how good a questionnaire is, or how blessed with interviewing skills someone might be, if the staff conducting the interview for employment have no first-hand experience of the work concerned, then they should not be doing the recruitment.

Often, unsuitable people are employed simply because the group doing the employing do not appreciate the intricacies of the job concerned.

Managers at the lowest levels should be involved when it comes to employing staff, it should never be left to personnel or senior management.

Any organisation, big or small, should hold employment boards consisting of either two or three people. At least one board member should be the future line manager of any prospective employee. Another member ought to be the line manager's supervisor. Those managers are not only on the board for their obvious expertise, but right from the start, a new employee can see their future supervisors have credibility and authority.

Job Histories

While on the subject of employment, many managers may seek advancement in another department or company. Therefore, a manager needs to know how to produce an attractive, eye catching, curriculum vitae [CV]. There are many formulas; the one I advocate is probably as good as any, it has ten headings and an appendix...

1. Full Name [*with a picture if possible*]

2. Date and Place of Birth

3. Status [*married/single and number of children, if applicable, state dependant or otherwise*]

4. Qualifications [*BA Hons: Diploma management studies; etc*]

5. Profile

A Profile should be an outline of what you are and what you have done in a few dynamic lines: it is an opportunity to catch the eye. How you write a profile depends on what job you are after, for instance:

Facts – You are an engineer who has managed a small steel construction company for three years. The company employs thirty people.

Job 1 applied for – *construction manager, large building company* – Profile: - Experienced in all aspects of construction both on sight and at the planning stage. Involved in managing the fabrication of the Forth Road Bridge plus the Blackpool Tower refurbishment [*see full history*].

Job 2 applied for – *Manager, large construction company* – Profile: - Experienced in all aspects of construction, [*Forth Road Bridge, Blackpool Tower refurbishment*] people management [*responsible for investors in people registration*] and administration of industrial organisations [*see summary and full history*].

Both profiles only consist of a few lines; they describe the same person but paint an initially diverse picture designed to catch the eye of people looking for different things. Reading the profile often decides if the summary and career history get a glance – it can literally be that brutal.

6. Employment Summary

The employment summary should be an historic record of every job you have ever had ie:

1990 – 1995 Blogs Ltd:
1995 – 2004 Acne Widgets & Co:

Obviously, leave the summary out if you have only had the one job, otherwise all it shows, rather graphically, is you are inexperienced and slightly bureaucratic.

7. Career History

A career history should start in reverse, ie: - your last job first. It should contain details of every post held, major tasks completed and any glowing reports or awards.

Not many prospective employers conducting an initial sift want to read a whole career history, just the up to date parts. By putting them first, you create a good initial impression.

8. Education, Qualifications and Training

Education, qualifications and training refer to three specific areas of your life. Education is obviously schooling and university. Qualifications could also be schooling, university, apprenticeship or certificated courses. Training refers to employment [*in-house*] courses and unqualified experience; remember an experienced worker with no formal qualifications can be more desirable than a person with the ink still wet on a newly awarded degree.

9. Miscellaneous

Miscellaneous covers everything that does not fit anywhere else but says something interesting about you ie: - 2002 – 2008 Member of St Harry's School Board of Governors etc.

10. Hobbies and Interests

Hobbies and interests are slightly more personal but also make a statement about who you are.

The last two headings will probably only be read if a company is very keen on you and competition is stiff. Never doubt their importance though; in a tight run contest, they could be the deciding factor.

Finally, a CV should contain an appendix with copies of all your qualifications... not the originals. Sounds obvious?

I once received an original masters degree with a CV in the post. It came complete with the following instructions... *'Just destroy it if you decide not to call me for interview...'*

Axioms To Help You Think

Some managers have lightening wit that can come up with a ready answer in any situation; the rest of us need some space and time to think.

Although I have a strong dislike for most politicians, one can learn from them when it comes to the art of saying a lot that declares absolutely nothing. They also have a knack of imparting horrendous details and making them sound alright.

Phrases that stall, placate or leave people smiling as they softly convey devastation, all without giving too much away, can be like gold dust in some situations:

- 'I hear everything you say…' [*Apparently, you are planning to give sympathetic consideration to someone's unreasonable or unclear demands*]

- 'You've obviously put a great deal of thought into this and it deserves no less respect from me… ' [*You are making it clear in the most diplomatic way possible that you will not be giving any direct answers instantaneously*].

- 'We're not far away from each other; we just need to kick it around for a bit longer…' [*I'm not giving in, so you can stew for a while until you finally accept my way of thinking*]

- 'By the way, I've been meaning to ask, how's the new baby?' [*This is a flexible question designed to bring up an irresistible change of subject dear to your opponent's heart when you are in a corner or need time to think immediately*]

- 'I'm sure you know there are a number of ways we could approach this situation...' [*I don't like any of your alternatives, think of another or I will*]

- 'We need to be very clear about exactly what the issues are...' [*I really don't have a clue what all of them are yet*]

- 'I think it's time for a comfort break...' [*If I don't get out of this meeting fast, I'm going to... or, I need time to think*]

- 'I think I'm fairly clear about the situation, but I'm just waiting until the final details emerge...' [*Time and help are needed*]

- 'Apparently superseding consequences have materialised and have been effusively engaged by the relevant departments but certain nuances are yet to emerge and therefore temporary postponement seems tolerable and logical...' [*Same as the last one but designed to be more impressive should the occasion require it*]

- 'There are always unforeseen shifts in market forces requiring rationalisations…' [*The latest product is a complete failure… or, some of them won't have a job at the end of the month and they can't say I didn't mention the fact*]

- 'Supply and demand are essentials of existence we simply cannot afford to discount...' [*Same as the one above but vaguer. Designed for those who already have an idea their days are numbered*]

- 'An unfamiliar outlook is always welcome and rarely tainted by the contempt of acquaintance...' [*We are being taken over… or, the new person's here to stay so make the best of it*].

You may think that the above axioms are a somewhat light-hearted or frivolous way to end a book on such a serious subject. Perhaps they are, I apologise if any of you feel aggrieved.

Consider this though; at times common sense dictates that diplomatic prudence may need to supersede the bare facts of blunt honesty.

Just never let anything compromise your personal standards or honour.

Always do your best; you are taking the money so be prepared to earn it. Conversely, never lose your sense of proportion. It appears we only have the one life, make sure it is filled with good things, not regrets.

www.ingramcontent.com/pod-product-compliance
Lightning Source LLC
Chambersburg PA
CBHW060845170526
45158CB00001B/239

*9 7 8 1 2 9 1 6 4 7 9 7 6 *